Better Homes and Gardens®

Remodeling
Idea File

Better Homes and Gardens® Books
Des Moines, Iowa

Better Homes and Gardens® Books
An imprint of Meredith® Books

Remodeling Idea File
Editor: Brian Kramer
Contributing Editors: Cynthia Pearson, Dan Weeks
Contributing Writers: Karin Baji Holms, Amber Barz, Jan Walker
Art Director: David Jordan
Copy Chief: Terri Fredrickson
Copy and Production Editor: Victoria Forlini
Editorial Operations Manager: Karen Schirm
Managers, Book Production: Pam Kvitne, Marjorie J. Schenkelberg
Contributing Copy Editor: Kim Catanzarite
Contributing Proofreaders: Erin McKay, Karen Schultz, Brenda Scott Royce
Indexer: Sharon Duffy
Electronic Production Coordinator: Paula Forest
Editorial and Design Assistants: Kaye Chabot, Karen McFadden, Mary Lee Gavin

Meredith® Books
Publisher and Editor in Chief: James D. Blume
Design Director: Matt Strelecki
Managing Editor: Gregory H. Kayko
Executive Editor, Home Decorating and Design: Denise L. Caringer

Director, Operations: George A. Susral
Director, Production: Douglas M. Johnston

Vice President and General Manager: Douglas J. Guendel

Better Homes and Gardens® Magazine
Editor in Chief: Karol DeWulf Nickell

Meredith Publishing Group
President, Publishing Group: Stephen M. Lacy
Vice President-Publishing Director: Bob Mate

Meredith Corporation
Chairman and Chief Executive Officer: William T. Kerr

Chairman of the Executive Committee: E. T. Meredith III

Inspiring Case Studies to Build Your Design Strategy

In your hands you hold the key to your home's next remodeling job, a fresh resource that's full of inspiration. The ***Better Homes and Gardens® Remodeling Idea File*** combines remodeling project case studies with tips, strategies, and information that help you customize your home to perfectly suit your needs and lifestyle. Chapters introduce you to remodeling options: Upgrade your interior with simple, fun facelifts. Finish existing space in basements and attics. Rework floor plans to create fresh, functional spaces. Bump up or out to make way for everything from a breakfast nook to a multiroom addition. Tip boxes throughout the book highlight ideas you can adapt to your own house, and Idea File sections in each chapter give you the lowdown on the latest techniques, materials, and strategies.

Use the home tour on the following four pages to jumpstart your remodeling imagination. You'll find design solutions both major and minor to transform your remodeling dreams into reality.

1 Two sets of arches balanced over columns gracefully separate kitchen from entry from gathering room in an addition that spans the length of a house. When viewed from one end, the repeated arches form a double frame for the stone fireplace in the distant gathering space.

2 Weighty light fixtures hang deep into the foyer, providing focal points and a touch of old-world warmth in the expansive, whitewashed cathedral-ceilinged space.

3 Informally laid new brick added to a pre-existing stucco arch-way gives the appearance of freshly uncovered masonry, perfectly in keeping with the original brickwork to the right. The arch serves as a transitional frame from rustic dining area to library beyond.

4 A jagged tub surround of Colorado flagstone echoes the shapes of the mountains just outside this ski slope home. Small windows and glass block walls keep light moving and bouncing at the lower levels while maintaining privacy; larger and monitor windows farther up the wall offer spectacular views and fill the room with sunlight. A hefty exposed beam breaks up the wall expanse.

5

1

2

1 Quirky yet clean-cut niches, cubbyholes, a fireplace, and a window seat add interest to this master bedroom. Positioned beneath the lift of a shed-style roof dormer, the room offers great views of the vistas beyond. Note the band-trimmed linen draperies and blinds that can be pulled or dropped for privacy. The transom windows over the headboard open to the hallway for ventilation.

2 A monitor—a raised roof style with low windows that was common in barn construction—draws in light and ventilation while maintaining privacy. Placed over a series of rooms that comprise a master suite, it adds considerable drama to the home inside and out. The decorative crosspieces between rooms echo the windows' divided panes.

3 *Floating display shelves climb a hearthside corner, echoing the rectangular shapes in the polished-stone fireplace. The room's clean, contemporary lines provide an ideal backdrop for showing off a huge print.*

4 *A curvaceous iron chandelier offers shapely contrast to the rectangular skylight with peaked windows. Both the chandelier and ample window trim add formality to the modern skylight.*

You know how it goes. . . . Sometimes when you're feeling dowdy, you don't need a new you or even a new body; you simply need some new clothes! That can be the case for houses too. Surface treatments, from counter-tops and paint to furnish-ings and windows in fresh shapes, go a long way to energize an existing home. The impact of a fresh look is great, the cost is far less than mov-ing into a new place, and the change may be all you need to fall in love with your home all over again. The case studies on the following pages prove this point. Check out the ho-hum house that was refreshed with French flair, cluttered places that

get slick solutions, a decrepit historic house that regains its original stature, and simple houses made lively with salvaged furnishings. Then roam your own house with an eye toward discovering possibilities. Turn the page for inspiring perspectives.

Redecorate

French Connection

Once a rambling patchwork of rooms with little character or continuity, this Oklahoma home now passes for a French farmhouse on the Normandy coast. Though the original 1920s log cabin was buried and butchered beyond recognition, a pair of avid Francophiles saw potential in its timber, which proved to be the right material for giving the house an overall new look.

The facade now boasts a harmonious blend of soft-colored stucco and half-timbers with vintage French casement windows that were salvaged from a farmhouse in France. The same look is replicated inside the house. While stucco is used in many architectural styles, it becomes classic French country when combined with recycled materials such as fanciful wrought iron, stone, or terra-cotta on floors, and honey-hued and painted woods as shown here.

The home's greatest transformation was achieved by removing the dropped ceilings to reveal rooflines that inspired several creative treatments, such as a rustic, shedlike canopy in the sunroom and vaulted, partially stuccoed and beamed ceilings elsewhere. All ceiling renovations were made with little change to the roofline; the only exception is a new entrance foyer that was raised to lot level and fitted with a salvaged French farmhouse door and stone surround.

Before

1 Salvaged shutters used as interior doors echo the texture of the sunroom's rough timber ceiling. Floor-to-ceiling French doors and windows replace run-of-the-mill sliders.

2 Large round log beams, salvaged from the cabin's original siding, combine with narrower, half-round logs for a textured master bedroom ceiling. French doors and windows were added, and a paneled wall, constructed from salvaged building parts, is painted the same white and finished to simulate an aged patina.

3 A raised entry foyer establishes a French farmhouse theme beneath a new vaulted ceiling beamed with old barn wood. Rustic stone flooring, yellow stucco walls, an old door with wrought iron hardware, and arched casement windows contribute to the style.

4 Earthy salvaged Mexican terra-cotta floor tiles ground airy floor-to-ceiling windows in the guest room. Here, recycled and painted lap siding covers the raised ceiling.

Raise *a Ceiling*

Nothing ensures drama like soaring spaces. From stucco to tongue-and-groove pine, half-round hewn timbers, steel beams, faux-painting, and even skylights, raised ceilings are ready and willing to receive a wide range of decorative materials and finishes. Your roof's construction affects your ability to remove an existing ceiling to reveal and finish the unused space above. Standard rafter-and-beam construction makes possible the ceiling treatments you see here. If prefabricated trusses hold up your roof, the cost of raising the ceiling may not be worth the result. (Take a look in your attic. A rafter-and-beam setup looks like an upside-down "V" or an "A." Trusses are pieces of lumber that zigzag from roof to ceiling joists.) If you choose to vault a ceiling, you limit options for concealing wiring. Partial ceilings (connecting two of the roof's several collar ties) offer a surface for hanging recessed light fixtures or hiding a ceiling fan's connections. Exposed beams also offer solutions for hanging light fixtures and ceiling fans, and concealing wiring.

Wide-Open
White

Case Study A sunlit soak in a deep claw-foot tub gets even better when, afterward, you can slip between crisp, white bedsheets just steps away. This true pleasure soak is in a master bedroom in a 1920s Southern California cottage. The decision to merge sleeping and bathing spaces—closeting the toilet only—follows a European model, where the lack of dividing walls implies greater intimacy. The open plan also allows for a lighter and brighter space, an important consideration in this coastal setting where homes are generally open to the outdoors.

The new double-duty master suite, located on the second story of a small addition, is the grand finale of

an extensive remodeling job. Craftsman cottages were originally designed as a series of small rooms to stay shady and cool; this one was remodeled to open it up to invite in sunlight and breezes. The new design lifted the ceilings to the rafters, bared the windows, and removed walls to enhance both air circulation and the flow of space.

A bright white palette—seen in room after room on walls and fabrics, and in the vintage-style gleaming porcelain bathroom—maximizes newly available light. Salvaged wooden doors, rustic cabinetry, and 100-year-old recycled floors help this renovated cottage retain the graceful patina of age.

1 New and antique linens—including a lace tablecloth—dress the bed in many shades of white. The trim on the reproduction Craftsman window is painted a shade brighter than the walls and salvaged plank ceiling.

2 Painted beaded-board wainscoting and vanity doors define the room's bathing zone.

3 Casually propped mirrors of different heights and shapes reflect light and help blend the transition from bathing area to sleeping area. White curtains hung on swing rods replace heavy closet doors for a look that's softer and lighter.

4 In the bath, a clear glass shower stall borrows sunlight that spills through a small window.

5 A combination of white paint and clear-coated wood lends interest to the simple square balusters and newel posts of the Craftsman staircase. Salvaged doors hide a storage nook tucked under the stairs.

Arts & Craftsmanship

Case Study Why sink time and dollars into a long-abandoned house? Particularly a house with a leaky roof, termites, crumbling plaster walls, a kitchen floor that had fallen through clear to the basement, and no working electricity, plumbing, or mechanicals? A love of fine craftsmanship and historic architecture proved reason enough for the buyers who saved this dilapidated Richmond, Virginia mansion.

Despite its treacherous condition, the house boasted brilliant but deteriorating examples of Arts and Crafts

1 *A wide-windowed entry, cheery pink paint and bright white trim lighten the timbered Tudor facade.*

2 *Restoration work focused on the once-fabulous but crumbling Arts and Crafts staircase. Others may have opted for something simpler in its place, but the owners chose to preserve the staircase, taking it apart, remitting many intricate pieces, strengthening and rebuilding it to its former glory.*

3 *Sparkling crystal pendants on a vintage wrought-iron chandelier draw attention upward to the staircase's elaborate millwork.*

4 *The dining room is splendidly dressed with a new French-limestone fireplace surround, a multipane garden door, and full, ballgown-like draperies. The moldings are original to the house.*

15

Old houses can be as comforting as old friends, but making the choice to rescue one from the brink of demolition is a serious commitment of time and effort, not to mention money. Before taking the plunge, you'll want to: (1) consult a structural engineer for a detailed report on the extent of the house's damage and its needed repairs; (2) research tax breaks that might alleviate repair costs; (3) seek temporary quarters (it is neither safe nor enjoyable to live with the construction of a major restoration); and (4) expect the unexpected—whether it's the joy of discovering an original fireplace behind drywall or the disappointment of realizing the restoration requires more patience and money than initially estimated.

After you make the decision to restore, set priorities. Period halls and salons are far more appealing than 100-year-old kitchens and baths. Some work you may choose to do yourself; other projects are best left to the educated instincts of a recommended restoration professional who is as familiar with today's construction resources as the building materials, styles, and techniques of yesteryear. To find qualified craftspeople, search directories for "Building Restoration and Preservation" or contact an architect or local historical preservation board for recommendations.

millwork and ornament. These include a Moravian Tileworks fireplace surround, coffered ceiling, arched portals, and intimate nooks lined with built-in bookcases. Restoring the living room, the dining room, and the foyer to their original grandeur became top priority. Along the way the house revealed structural flaws (and the inevitable expenses that come with them) that required the dismantling of many features including the house's greatest feat of Arts and Crafts design—a showstopping staircase with open, paneled soffits and intricate stepped railing (see page 14). The staircase was rebuilt and incorporates some original parts as well as remilled pieces that replace those too far gone.

In this case, period accuracy was important with regard to the bones of each room—moldings, ceilings, floors, doors, and windows—but was less so when it came to painting walls, choosing carpets, and designing draperies. Such elements were used to put a personal stamp on the home, bypassing the frozen-in-time approach to period home restoration.

5 *The living room's tile fireplace surround is now restored minus its original mantel. Craftsmen milled a new one, replicating designs of the era. They also re-created the arch for the hearth's cozy inglenook to replace the rotted original.*

6 *An abundance of rich fabric, Baroque architectural ornamentation, and faux-aged walls soften the sharp angles of the living room's restored coffered ceiling and entryway of divided-light windows and doors.*

Face Value

Case Study A shingled fisherman's cottage near Maryland's Chesapeake Bay was revived in just two months with little more than new windows, floors, a few cans of paint, and a clever reshuffling of space. Each easy fix focused on emphasizing the cottage's single best asset—its lush riverfront site.

The 80-year-old cottage sits on prime real estate. But before the renovation, tiny windows and the lack of a comfortable room from which to enjoy the river view meant the cottage failed to do its location justice. Local codes prohibited building toward the river; a screened-in porch and part of a concrete patio were converted into a new windowed sitting room, now called the "river room." Using the same tall, multi-light windows and French doors opens up the rear addition on the facade as well. There, an existing vestibule received an airy rehab. Removing its dropped ceiling and a

Before   **After**

portion of its interior wall transformed the space from a cramped pass-through hall into a full-fledged room with ample space for sitting or greeting guests.

Antiquing Kitchen Cabinetry

A faux-antique surface requires painting in layers: You must distress the top coat to simulate years of everyday wear that exposes an earlier color coat underneath.

The technique is a three-step process: Apply a base color in a gloss or semigloss finish for easy cleaning; repaint with a second color in a similar finish (mustard yellow here); and once dry, use sand papers of various coarseness or subject the piece to gentle denting, scratching, and gouging with rings of keys, coins, or even lengths of chain to reveal the undercoat in high-wear areas such as door edges, corners, and handles.

For added decorative effect add smooth layers of a third color over some drawer fronts (in this kitchen, creamy white) and distress them, or add painted country stencils or a contrasting trim. You can protect the finish with a coat of polyurethane, but it will prevent further wear—and charm.

1 Colorful draperies frame river views in this light-filled sitting room, which replaces a laundry room, screen porch, and patio.

2 A second doorway eases the flow of traffic from the living room to the kitchen. The layout remains unchanged, but period-style running shelves, a ceramic tile countertop, and the cabinets' faux-antique finish add further charm and interest at minimal expense.

3 The renovation lightened and brightened the vestibule with a raised ceiling, a new French door, and six muntined casement windows. Moderately priced vinyl floor tiles pass for grouted stone, while sunny yellow-tinted beaded boards and vintage red metal garden chairs establish the cottage's color scheme.

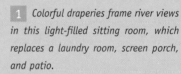

Before

19

Reduced to
Elegance

1 In the living area natural tones and textures balance sleek, clean-lined furnishings and contemporary surfaces with comfortable warmth. One oversize painting emphasizes the wall's generous expanse.

2 A windowsill display of tall grasses in translucent blue vases draws eyes upward to the room's soaring ceilings.

3 A built-in closet spanning the dining area was torn out in favor of more floor space and room for a handcrafted pine cupboard. Attractive chair backs, a carved wooden screen from Bali, the steel drum, and a fishing net-cum-chandelier play off the smooth warm surfaces of walls, ceilings, floors, and countertops.

4 Thanks to a previous remodeling project that raised the ceiling, the duplex needed only small structural changes to enable light's easy flow throughout.

Case Study Re-creating a space is often as much about making reductions as additions. With 12-foot ceilings and two terraces in the trees, this light-filled, 1,000-square-foot Seattle duplex was ripe for a loftlike transformation. Its homeowner, a professional space planner, was quick to see the possibilities and the obstacles between the existing place and an open, flowing space.

A wrecking bar and hammer helped yank out protruding half-walls and built-ins that chewed into valuable floor space. Closets were also removed, adding as much as 3 feet to the length of rooms. Maximizing space was not enough, however. Further ensuring the home's visual flow meant clearing surfaces—walls, floors, ceilings, and countertops—of obstructions both large and small. That included an awkwardly placed window and bookcase on the living room wall, which made way for an expansive, smooth surface ideal for hanging contemporary art. An ordinary half-brick mantel was remodeled by facing the entire fireplace wall with a surround of weathered steel sheeting. An abundance of recessed lights (whose holes cut up ceilings) were ripped out, plugs and switches relocated from eye level to more discreet hiding places. The furnishings palette was edited as carefully as the loft's shape. Natural colors and materials now predominate, creating textural interest while weaving walls, floors, and furnishings into a harmonious whole. Most fabrics and carpets are solid in color to minimize visual clutter, and furniture sits on uncovered legs leaving as much floor visible as possible. The result: Rooms that feel more spacious and sleeker, without a change to the duplex's cozy dimensions.

Metal *Fireplace Surrounds*

Surrounding the traditional hearth with sheets of industrial steel puts a contemporary spin on any interior—whether you choose a slick, silver gloss finish, a primitive rusty red, or the toasty mix of coppers and browns featured in this Seattle home's acid-washed steel surround. If you like the metal approach, you also can create a surround using copper, tin, or galvanized steel. All are low in cost, but their size and weight sometimes make installation labor intensive. Dedicated do-it-yourself types can search the Yellow Pages under "Steel Fabricators" for price quotes on materials, delivery, and installation, but such a job is generally best coordinated by an architect or building contractor who can ensure compliance with local building and fire codes.

A 7-gauge ($^3/_{16}$") piece of sheet metal around the firebox on a 10x12-foot wall can weigh as much as 900 pounds and range from $6,000 to $10,000 installed (higher for stainless steel). Using 10 gauge ($^1/_8$") might lower the material cost slightly but would have little effect on the price of labor. Copper is the most economical choice of metals and is the easiest to install. Available in sheets as thin as $^1/_{16}$" (.0216 gauge), lightweight copper can be mounted using adhesives and screws at a cost of $2,000-$3,000 for professional installation and less if you do it yourself.

Little House,
Big Charm

Case Study Glamour once flitted in and out of this tiny 700-square foot California bungalow when it served as a dressing space for a nearby film studio. But more recently it was a characterless rental property of boxy little rooms and low ceilings. That changed when an interior decorator made it her home and transformed the once-drab property with a plentiful mix of eclectic furnishings, fabrics, and antiques.

Decorative touches were favored over raising ceilings or installing new windows. Large furnishings boost the appeal of the small rooms and visually play with the scale of the space. Pretty but suitably overscaled fabric patterns, such as big-bloom florals and large-repeat Damascus prints, were selected for both their impact and their ability to make small spaces feel cozy. A scattering of playful objects and accessories, many of them mere flea market castoffs,

From Trash to Treasure

Decorating with salvage is less about finding one-of-a-kind objects than flexing your creative muscle so you can see the potential in something that others cast off. The back of a porch swing makes wonderful wall art; a silver teapot becomes a lovely light fixture. In this California house, a birdcage-plus-chandelier floor lamp yields greater charm than the sum of its parts.

Invention is the key to salvage success, not the number or value of objects you acquire. Unfocused flea market binges only bring clutter. To sort trash from treasure, take these tips for using salvage to the greatest decorative advantage:

- Imagine a location in your home for each piece you buy.
- Think past the object's traditional uses to the different functions its shape or form suggests.
- Don't be afraid to alter an object or to merge the old with the new.
- Shop with confidence. This isn't like antiquing—you don't need the expertise of a professional dealer, you only need to know what you like.
- Don't be swayed by the market. Texture, color, and craftsmanship are more important considerations than an object's rarity, price, or provenance.

are displayed as found or repurposed to inventive ends. One-of-a-kind charm was the decorative goal. A bright, faux fireplace and rooms in moody, decorative washes of saturated garden hues give the little house energy and glow. Like the weathered patina on vintage furniture, these gently mottled walls display worn beauty that projects a storybook cottage look, a nostalgic juxtaposition of old and new, dressy and primitive, pristine and distressed.

1 A bright blue front door calls attention to hollyhocks, delphiniums, and foxgloves.

2 A sofa, casual pine-plank coffee table, and salvaged hotel sign set a casual mood in the small living room. A faux-painted fireplace creates a storybook feel while floral draperies hung over bamboo blinds conjure visions of English Country gardens.

3 The playful combination of a fancy chandelier and an old birdcage stand sheds light on the room's romantic features: soft blue walls, children's book illustration prints, and a curvy oversize headboard with floral flourishes.

4 Vintage floral fabrics from the 1940s dress windows as well as shelves. The display cabinet is actually an old icebox, with its upper doors removed.

5 An enormous mirror, hung horizontally to span the width of a bedroom wall, visually enlarges the room.

Renew with Windows

New windows are a savvy way to brighten the mood of your home, enhance its sense of space, or increase its architectural character. Thoughtfully placed windows encase views of a garden, treetops, or cityscape much the way the perfect frame complements a fine painting. Windows also add subtlety and dimension to a room by enabling the play of sunlight and shadows on different textures and tones.

For the budget-wise remodeler, new windows offer vast possibilities for reinventing a space without the time and expense of a full renovation. If your home is functional but has a dark, cramped feel, the problem may be due to small and widely spaced windows. Similarly expansive

1 A patterned mix of rectangular, square, and triangular glass panes opens up the entire facade of this sophisticated lodge-style retreat to its lakeside view, helping to emphasize the synergy between the room's treetop location and its soaring vaulted ceiling.

2 Variations on a theme unify the windows and doors of this dining nook, where muntins divide the glass panes into a rhythmic geometric pattern. The eye-catching design opens the room to the outdoors, while de-emphasizing a less-than-spectacular suburban view.

spaces feel cold and oppressive when they're closed off from the outdoors and dependent on artificial light.

Whether you're thinking of dropping in solid walls of glass, creating geometric designs in existing walls, or replacing older, smaller windows with larger versions of the same style, recent advances in window technology work for you. Windows require

less maintenance, are more energy efficient, and offer a wider selection of types and styles than ever before. Here are a few things to keep in mind as you shop for your new windows:

Match your home's architecture. If you're just replacing or adding a few windows, match the type, style, and size of the windows to the originals so the two blend.

Renew with Windows

Consider your options. New windows are available with features such as low-E coatings, which reduce heat gain, heat loss, and fabric fading; multipane and argon-filled glass, which greatly increases a window's insulation value; and vinyl- and aluminum-clad frames that never need scraping or painting. Other convenient features include tilting sashes and removable grilles, which make cleaning easier.

Consider a window's lifetime cost. If you're planning to live in your house for some time, consider the lifetime cost when replacing or installing a window, not just the initial cost. Lifetime cost includes installation, cleaning, maintenance, and energy costs. A top-of-the-line window—for instance, a vinyl-clad wood unit with a tilting sash and low-E-coated glass—usually costs twice what an economy-grade wood unit without the tilting sash, low-E coating, and vinyl cladding does. The "expensive" window costs no more to install, is much cheaper to maintain, and saves energy, more than recouping its higher initial investment over time. In addition, high-quality windows are a plus when you decide to sell your home.

1 The double-hung windows in this home office are designed to be enjoyed from both inside the house and out. Muntins on the top window frame maintain the Arts and Crafts character of the home; the undivided glass below offers clear views and prevents distracting shadows on the desktop.

2 A tall stack of transom windows painted crisp white transform a breakfast nook in the kitchen into a poolside sunroom. A triple-lighted door blends into the design, thanks to careful attention to proportions, matching trim, and three molding strips mounted at the height of each transom.

3 Multiple layers of recessed molding and trim on each transom window add depth to the framed view beyond.

4 Muntins update the original, massive, solid-pane picture window of a 1950s ranch house.

This chapter shows what you can accomplish if you step up your remodeling ambitions and do some interior rearranging as well as cosmetic refreshing. These case studies go beyond surface treatments. They include renovations that required such things as moving appliances and built-in features, redirecting the traffic flow within or between rooms, judiciously removing a non-load-bearing wall or two to expand or reconfigure interior space, and even completely rearranging a floor plan.

As this chapter shows, the results can be dramatic. Yet because the overall footprint of the house stays the same, the costs remain modest compared to those for a major addition. If you have enough room—but just not the *right kind* of room for the way you live—rearranging may offer what you need to suit both your lifestyle and your budget.

Even if you're thinking about building an addition, take a close look at this chapter. You may be surprised to find the solution you need within the walls of the home you already have.

Rearrange

About Face

Case Study This project turned a boring shoebox of a ranch into a stylish modern bungalow, from the inside out. The renovation flip-flopped the floor plan, shifted the entrance, renovated the interior, and refurbished and relandscaped the exterior. The house gained a sense of spaciousness, drama, and flow, and great views of the outside. The great-room allows for convivial family living and a view of the yard, so keeping an eye on playing children is a breeze.

Originally the home's front door opened directly into a small living and dining area beside a cramped kitchen. A cluster of bedrooms came next, followed by a modest family room at the back of the house—far too distant from the kitchen.

The new floor plan converted the living area and kitchen at the front of the home into a spacious master suite. Doing so allowed the family room in the back of the house to expand into space formerly occupied by a small bedroom and bath. The vaulted ceiling of the resulting great-room makes the large space feel even larger. The room includes a contemporary kitchen with an open design that keeps the cook in touch with family and friends.

1 The new design sacrificed a former bedroom and bath to create this spacious new living area. It features a vaulted ceiling, exposed rafters, and a wall of glass.

2 With its snack bar and open design, the new kitchen frees the cook from isolation and offers space for casual dining as well as a spot for the computer.

3 The master bedroom, formerly the living/dining room, features a tiny-but-functional office tucked into the former front stoop.

4 The master bath has high windows for privacy. A cozy bump-out makes space for a whirlpool tub.

5 The master suite now faces the street. A portion of the front stoop was enclosed to create an office. The gate on the right leads to a private courtyard and the new main entrance.

Outside *Options*

Major changes to your floor plan may mandate exterior changes as well.

Moving a main entry requires changing landscaping that redirects callers to the entry door. In this project flower beds bar the paths to the original entry, and a side gate beckons visitors.

While you're at it consider the new relationship of your reconfigured rooms to your yard. A raised patio and French doors here add outdoor living space to the master suite.

When you move or eliminate a garage door, remove your driveway also. Consider transforming the drive into a series of landscaped patios and walkways.

Finally, moving a bedroom to the front of a house may mandate more insulation and soundproofing to muffle traffic noise.

31

Beside the Beach

A beautiful beachside location on Delaware Bay proved to be the main selling point for this Victorian summer cottage. Built in 1905 and badly altered several times before being rescued by the current project, the house is a great example of how working within the box to reconfigure space works magic inside even when the goal is to preserve historic lines outside.

Here the key to the house's rebirth was its wraparound porch. The charming original feature had been awkwardly enclosed with cheap storm windows and a waist-high wall. The project removed an interior wall and annexed a portion of the porch as main living space.

Now the expanded lower level makes a visual leap toward the sea. Careful detailing retains a porchlike feel with a ceiling that features exposed joists and beaded board, both of which sport lines that pull

your eyes toward the ocean horizon. The renovation replaced several load-bearing walls with posts and exposed, vintage-style beams (see sidebar *right*), opening the entire interior to the views and making it comfortable for family get-togethers.

Other improvements include a relocated kitchen overlooking the beach and living areas; removing a wall between the new kitchen and living area and replacing it with a counter for casual dining; and a new deck off the master bedroom, a great place to lounge and take in the view.

The remaining porches were restored to their formal splendor, complete with new-but-original railings that create an outdoor living area overlooking the beach.

The exterior of the house was also restored. In addition to the porch detailing, restorers discovered and exposed original fish-scale shingles underneath asbestos siding.

1 Fish-scale shingles, a bumped-out second-story window, charming porch, and classic white-picket fence add up to a restored Victorian cottage by the sea.

2 A small entry hall offers a spot for kicking off shoes and hanging beach hats or the dog's leash. The fish-scale wall was originally part of the house's exterior.

3 The renovation moved the kitchen forward, into a space that had been part of the wraparound porch. Posts and beams replace load-bearing interior walls; the porch's new fir-strip floor blends with the original wood of the dining- and living-room floors.

Before

Removing Load-Bearing Walls

Conventional wisdom says not to tear down load-bearing walls unless necessary, as the complexity and the expense is considerably more than removing nonbearing partition walls. After load-bearing walls come down, you are left with the engineering problem of transferring the building's weight to a new load-bearing wall in a different location.

This project, however, was a case where removing walls was exactly what the remodeling doctor ordered. Otherwise the house's chief asset—its wonderful beach views—wouldn't be visible from much of the interior.

Fortunately a smart, simple solution eliminated much of the job's complexity: Load-bearing walls simply were replaced with posts and beams in the same places the original walls had been. The result: an open interior, with minimal reengineering required. Best of all the exposed posts and beams complement the exposed ceiling joists, giving the home an informal, gazebo-like charm.

3

1 Ceiling joists scraped of paint, warm wood floors, and an absence of partition walls unify the living and dining spaces in this 1905 beach house.

2 A new dormer houses the combination tub and shower in the master bathroom. The cabinet doors, actually recycled shutters, add to the house's relaxed beach style. A window over the tub provides natural light and architectural interest while retaining privacy.

3 A frosted, glazed pocket door between the bedroom and bath saves space, shares light, and preserves privacy.

4 Sliding glass doors open the master bedroom to a cedar deck built above a porch that provides spectacular second-story views of the ocean.

Before

Free-Flowing
Privacy

Case Study A recent remodeling of this modest suburban ranch house called for the merger of three rooms: a 12×15-foot master bedroom, an 8×10-foot master bath and a 12×11½-foot guest bedroom. The result is an airy, pampering master retreat that accommodates sleeping, dressing, bathing, primping, and watching television. Most activities are zoned by partial walls that stop several feet short of the ceiling, letting light find its way through the entire suite.

The retreat's design visually separates some spaces yet allows for long views that create a sense of expansiveness and flow. Color and window placement also play a key role in the design: Tall openings in white perimeter walls help bounce light into the room's center, while seven subtly contrasting hues accent partitions.

A key feature of the retreat is a low double-duty wall that separates the sleeping and dressing areas. One side of the wall functions as a headboard, the other is a display case. In a similar back-to-back situation, mirrors over the bathroom's double vanity hang from the back of freestanding closets.

Define *with Color*

Color offers a quick and easy means to control space perception: A single color—or family of similar colors—visually links spaces; contrasting colors separate them.

This suite, for instance, uses several different earthy colors—all of them warm yet neutral tones—on partition walls, shelving, cabinetry, and fabrics. The colors are distinct enough to carve zones for varying functions (sleeping, dressing, and bathing) from the airy white-painted surround of the perimeter walls and ceiling. Yet their contrast is subtle enough to create a pleasing flow—an important consideration with respect to open floor plans and the long sight lines that go with them.

Tip: To choose the perfect palette of neutral paint colors, select earthy tones that match the warmth or coolness of the accent colors you plan to include in furniture or decorative accessories. For example, the honey-toned shelving and cabinetry suggested warmer, red- and yellow-based neutrals.

1 *The unassuming appearance of this suburban ranch offers no hint of the extensively reworked floor plan within; yet the clean exterior geometry provides cues for the sleek furnishings and modular layout inside.*

2 *The rounded backside of the headboard wall makes a handsome display for books and a collection of American Craft pottery. Placed directly opposite a bank of closets, the cabinet's gentle arc and its homey display transform an otherwise empty corridor into an attractive dressing area.*

3 *Built-in drawers in the bathroom store clothes; mirrored closet doors and multiple windows keep the area bright for dressing.*

4 *An open hallway offers a clear view from one end of the master suite to the other. The space gains a great sense of depth as your eye moves through the sequence of open and closed spaces.*

5 *The warm eggplant color of the headboard wall cozies the sleeping area. The gray-painted storage unit partially blocks light and casts restful shadows. In the background, partition structures of varying heights and hues give the suite a layered look.*

6 *Versatile natural maple cabinetry combines storage, display, and media space to compensate for wall space given to French doors and windows.*

37

Let There Be Light

The biggest challenge of living in a rowhouse is how to get enough natural light to the home's interior so you don't feel as though you're living in a tunnel. At the same time the long, boxy floor plan begs for definition: Without the character of interesting shapes and angles to demarcate different rooms, it needs something to signal what each space is for.

This Washington, D.C., rowhouse is a great example of using interior architecture—partial walls,

interior windows, moldings, and a small bump-out—to give definition to three distinctly different spaces within a boxcarlike floor plan, while letting the maximum amount of natural light penetrate deep into the house.

In this case the living room, with its elegant bay window, was left intact. The work focused on the back of the house, where a tiny kitchen and den walled off the dining room, blocking

the center of the house from light and views. The new plan pulled down the walls and gave the kitchen

the run of the back of the house. A new bump-out stretches the kitchen just enough to house the range and some cabinetry. As a result it increases the window area and is the centerpiece of a new deck.

Meanwhile partial interior walls between the kitchen, family/dining, and living rooms give each space definition and character. Each wall is perforated by interior windows, which add architectural interest and share natural light. Closets and storage space line the windowless interior walls in both the kitchen and the dining room, hiding clutter and elegantly housing entertainment equipment. New moldings throughout add understated refinement to the vintage home's character.

From Awkward to Elegant

1. Salvaged cabinets and a vintage wood floor—formerly hidden under layers of shag carpet—grace the living room.

2. The house's good bones are visible in this Before shot. The featureless bump on the side is now a porch; the entry moved to the front.

3. The handsome, gabled facade begged for a street-facing front entry. A salvaged door and new portico look original.

4. What this house didn't need was one more tiny bedroom. This one—placed off the living room and far from a bath—became a sunny front foyer.

5. This screened porch replaces the former side entry, creating a spacious outdoor room. A beaded-board ceiling with exposed joists lends a vintage feel to the new space.

Before

Case Study A warren of tiny rooms combined with lots of wasted space and an awkward floor plan plagued this turn-of-the-century house in lakeside Sawyer, Michigan. In spite of its gracious facade, the entrance was on the featureless side of the house. Inside resided a small bedroom off the living room—as far as could be from the downstairs bath. Upstairs a huge hallway to nowhere claimed much of the floor space, shoving a diminutive bath and bedroom into far corners.

The home's remodeling is a textbook example of how to update an historic house into the more livable floor plan it should have had from the beginning. All this while enhancing its vintage feel without moving beyond the existing exterior walls.

The first step entailed the installation of a vintage front door in the window opening of the downstairs front-corner bedroom, turning that room into an entry foyer and giving the facade a welcoming focal point: a street-facing entry, complete with front steps and portico.

Next the upstairs hall was reclaimed as living space. Some of its square footage was apportioned to an enlarged bath that spans the back of the house, some to a master bedroom that nearly doubled in size, with a new closet.

Other changes included adding an island to the existing kitchen, thereby expanding counter space significantly without adding any square footage. A new side yard screen porch for relaxing and outdoor entertaining replaced the old entry, and a sunporch to the rear of the house was weatherized into an all-season sunroom. New vintage-look materials here and throughout the house lend their timeless, classic mood to this pristine restoration.

Wood Floors

Wood floors are increasingly popular throughout the house thanks to new finishes that make them an easy-care, durable choice. Although wood is more expensive to install than carpet or vinyl, it usually lasts for decades.

Your choices in wood and wood-like floors are three, presented in order of expense: laminate, solid wood, and engineered wood.

Laminate wood floors feature four-ply construction: 1) a backing or balancing layer, 2) a moisture-resistant wood-based core of high- or medium-density fiberboard, 3) a decorative layer that's a photograph of wood grain, and 4) a wear-resistant layer of melamine resins. These floors are similar in concept to laminate countertops, but the wear layer is further strengthened by hard particles.

Generally laminate wood floors are installed as floating floors. Planks—about ⅓-inch thick—are glued or snapped together and placed over a subfloor of vinyl, concrete, or wood. They're durable and great choices for high-traffic locations. Damaged planks can't be refinished, but they can be replaced, and putty is available for repairs. Unlike solid or engineered wood, laminate's cost doesn't vary according to wood variety. Cost is about $5–$10 per square foot installed.

Solid wood floors are generally ¾-inch thick. You can protect wood floors with surface finishes or penetrating finishes. With surface finishes, a water-based polyurethane forms a protective layer; on the other hand, penetrating finishes (usually tung oil) go deep into the wood surface to create a coating. You can feel

the wood grain through them. The look that results is usually a satin or slightly worn matte finish. Solid wood floors most often are finished on site and range from $6–$12 per square foot installed. Scuffs and dents—even stains—actually enhance their beauty. Eventually, when the surface progresses from "distressed" to just plain "worn bare," the wood

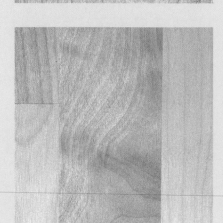

Old *Wood*

Remodelers seek salvaged or antique lumber pulled from old buildings, barns, and even gymnasiums to create aged, distressed looks. You have to do a little hunting to find what you want, so hop on the Internet and talk to contractors and salvage experts. Old flooring is hard to beat for beauty, but don't expect to find bargains as lots of handling is involved: finding it, removing it, and pulling nails.

Strips range from 1½-2¼ inches. Planks are wider than 2¼ inches. Parquet floors create patterns with shorter wood strips and tiles.

Wood Floors Are Easy

The high-maintenance waxing that accompanied wood floors is long gone. Solid, engineered, and laminate wood floors need nothing more than sweeping to limit damage from dirt, sand, and grit. Use a broom; the brush/beater bars on most vacuum sweepers actually dent a floor's finish. Place rugs and floor mats at your entrances to trap grit; shake them out often. Wipe up spills and foot tracks as they happen. If your floor's finish is in good shape, you can lightly damp-mop it with a neutral-pH wood cleaner or a product recommended by the floor's manufacturer.

Every three to five years, you may need to recoat urethane-finished floors in high-traffic areas. This is best done by a professional because it involves cleaning and lightly abrading the worn surface before applying fresh coats of urethane finish.

Keep floors that are protected with a penetrating finish swept clean and free of grit, dust, and dirt as well. Reapply tung oil to the entire floor surface or high-traffic areas only every 5–10 years.

Waxing a tung-oiled floor is a high-maintenance task. You need to strip it and rewax once or twice a year. Wipe spills quickly and never use water on it, as water leaves white spots.

Smart moves: Leave spiky heels, golf shoes, and bike cleats at the door to avoid denting the floor. Keep your pets' nails trimmed and filed. Slide pieces of felt between furniture legs and the floor.

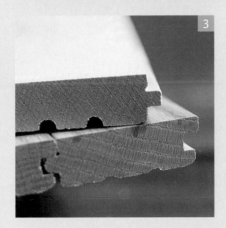

can be sanded and refinished to look like new again—an option that laminate and engineered wood floors can't offer.

Engineered wood is composed of three to five layers of wood stacked and glued together under heat and pressure. Wood expands and contracts with exposure to heat and humidity. The layers of engineered wood keep this activity to a minimum. With proper moisture-proofing and subfloor preparation, you can lay engineered wood where solid wood cannot be laid, such as over concrete and in high-moisture spaces. Engineered wood is generally factory-finished, which is considered by many to be superior to on-site finishing, and costs $8–$14 per square foot installed. Factory-finished floors install without hassle, odor, or dust. Unlike site-finished floors, they're ready to walk on as soon as they're installed.

Soft wood or hard? Despite protective finishes, dropped items and spiky heels can dent a wood floor. Hickory, pecan, hard maple, and oak are the hardest species, followed by white ash, beech, yellow birch, green ash, walnut, cherry, and mahogany. Pine is a soft wood, so avoid using it on floors that get hard use unless you prefer a distressed look. An exception: The heartwood of old-growth Southern yellow long-leaf pine is as tough as oak.

[1] *Laminate floors feature a top layer that's made of the same materials as laminate countertops—but they're 10 times as tough to take the punishment a kitchen floor gets day in and day out. Many are guaranteed for decades. Some install without glue, speeding installation time and ensuring tight, even joints. Finishes mimic a wide variety of wood species.*

[2] *Engineered wood floors are available in tongue-and-groove planks and feature the look and feel of a genuine hardwood surface. Because veneer is relatively thin, it can't be sanded and refinished like solid wood floors.*

[3] *Solid-sawn hardwood, like these oak planks, make up the most traditional type of wood floor. Moderate cost, lasting durability, a choice of finishes, and the ability to sand and refinish these floors have garnered them a popular reputation.*

[4] *Inexpensive and good-looking, pine has been used for floors for centuries. Easily dented, marred, and scratched, though, it's best used either in low-traffic areas or where a worn, distressed look is desired.*

Sometimes you simply can't get the living space you want—at least, not within the existing finished space in your home. No worries! You probably have some unfinished space—such as a basement, attic, porch, breezeway, or garage—that you can annex and convert into finished, four-season space. So before you raise the roof or pour the footings for a new addition's foundation, consider turning square footage you already have into the living space that you desire.

Not only is converting your unfinished space generally cheaper and easier than building new space, the process poses other advantages as well. Because you're working within your home's existing footprint, you won't gobble up additional yard space. And often you'll discover that spaces like attics and breezeways have architectural character that imparts an informal, even quirky charm to your new living space.

Browse through the case studies that follow, then take a good, hard look at your entire house. See whether you can work—in your own home—the same kind of alchemy that characterizes what you see on the following pages.

Remake

Breeze in and Stay Awhile

Case Study The back of this contemporary Texas home featured an open-air breezeway that connected the main body of the house to an above-garage apartment, a situation that was fine until the apartment's tenant moved out. The owners decided they'd rather have a family room for casual entertaining than an apartment to house strangers.

The apartment was a snap to convert. The space already had its own bathroom and, with large windows affording treetop views on all sides, it made a great gathering spot. Because it has a kitchenette, the space naturally doubles as a guest suite. The real trick was to convert the breezeway—formerly a dumping ground for boots, shoes, and other outdoor gear—into an enclosed space that makes for a welcoming transition into the reclaimed second-floor room.

To convert the passage into an inviting year-round room, the project replaced screening with new board-and-batten siding, lots of windows, French doors that lead to a rear deck, and a skylight. The stairs to the new family room were widened, and the entire space brightened up with a wash of white paint. A seating arrangement gives visitors a place to rest, and a rustic cabinet swallows clutter. To keep the room temperate, a ceiling fan cools the space on hot Texas days, and insulation beneath keeps the floor warm on cool days. (In cooler climates, you'll want to insulate walls and ceilings as well.)

Before

1 This sunny former breezeway leads upstairs to an apartment-turned-family-room. A shutter screen at the top of the stairs conceals a kitchenette.

2 Dark siding, beams, and unfinished wood stairs gave the former breezeway a gloomy aspect, so the space was rarely used. The breezeway is now sunnier than before, thanks to lots of windows, glass doors, and a new skylight.

3 The gathering room itself is perfectly suited for casual entertaining with leather sofas and club chairs. Bamboo shades filter light and provide privacy when the space serves as a guest suite.

4 The enticing outdoor deck sees a lot more action now that the passage has been transformed.

5 A reclaimed barn-stall door slides on tracks, closing off the new family room from the stairway and porch below. The door provides a visual link to the home's rural Texas setting and the room's views of the adjacent stuble, paddock, and horses.

From Garage to
Gracious Gathering

Case Study The only thing that this 1940s brick Atlanta home lacked was casual living space. An inviting gathering room was attained by tapping the two-stall garage just off the kitchen. Now the former car shelter is a comfortable 20×20-foot family area, while a new garage on the opposite side of the house protects automobiles.

Two robust pillars provide a graceful transition from breakfast room to family room. The pillars replace the load-bearing wall that previously separated kitchen from garage (see the sidebar about load-bearing walls on page 33). What was once the garage door wall is now a grand yet functional focal point composed of a fireplace, built-in shelving, and roomy cabinets. Sidewalls feature a host of windows: One faces the patio and has a bank of five double-hungs, the other has two windows that align with the first and last windows of the bank opposite them. Overhead, the sides of a cathedral ceiling follow the roof's pitch; underfoot, oak floors flow from kitchen through family gathering space. The result? A handsome often-used dwelling.

Changes to the original garage exterior appear minor. The bank of double-hungs offers views of the patio (installed prior to the garage conversion). New siding and a chimney replace the wall that previously housed the overhead garage door.

Garage Conversion Pros and Cons

When you're pressed for living space, it may be tempting to convert the garage from car shelter to living room, office, bedroom, or workshop. Several factors make garage conversions attractive, yet other factors make them impractical, even undesirable. Weigh all factors before committing to a garage conversion.

Pros:

• Garage walls and roofs usually are structurally sound and need nothing more than additional insulation and finish drywall.

• Floors usually are lower than adjoining floors, making it a cinch to install a clean, level subfloor and new finish flooring material.

Cons:

• If you don't plan to build a new garage, you need to find another place to park the cars and store all the stuff you previously stashed in the garage.

• You also need to rework the garage exterior so it matches your house—a costly but necessary measure.

• You'll have to rip up and redirect the driveway and have the yard beneath it landscaped. If you don't, visitors may drive right up to your new living space.

• If you don't replace the garage with a new one or make these revisions, the value of your property potentially can take a nose-dive. So proceed with caution!

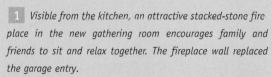

1 Visible from the kitchen, an attractive stacked-stone fire place in the new gathering room encourages family and friends to sit and relax together. The fireplace wall replaced the garage entry.

2 To replace the old garage, a new tuck-under garage topped with a porch is positioned on the right side of the house.

3 A bank of windows opens the great-room to views of the paved patio, which existed before the conversion. Steps rising from the patio to the house provide plenty of interest. The former garage door wall is freshly sided and landscaped.

4 To the right of the fireplace, cabinet doors slide back to reveal a television. A base within the cabinet lifts the TV to comfortable viewing height.

Under the
Eaves

Case Study Rather than remodeling out, consider remodeling up. The extra space you need may be right above your head.

This house gained a bedroom, a sitting room that doubles as an additional bedroom, and a bath—all carved out of an attic that sports a cozy, rustic character all its own.

The main requirement for an attic remodel is height. If the attic has plenty of height at the ridgepole, usually you can add dormers to take care of headroom elsewhere. The dormers here add more than light and space. By placing a twin bed into each of two dormers in the bedroom, separate sleeping spaces were created with visiting grandchildren in mind. Beds, dressers, and a chaise are tucked cozily into under-the-eaves nooks, maximizing both space and charm. Two pocket doors lead from each room to the hall, allowing for openness or privacy, as needed.

The loftlike geometry of the space inspired use of salvaged barn beams and boards throughout. The look is further embellished with vintage horse- and dog-themed accessories. The homeowner in this case wanted the attic space to have personality so the grandchildren would want to come out and stay at grandma's house.

Mission accomplished. Now the bigger question is, how do you get them to go back home?

Big *Views*

A floor-to-ceiling window can provide the "wow" factor in any renovation—and is particularly effective in an attic, where the room's elevation makes the most of the view. When choosing big windows for a project:

Keep things in proportion. Make sure your house visually supports a big window.

Stay in stylistic sync. Choose a window that complements your home's architecture.

Provide for ventilation. Many large windows are stationary, so flank them with smaller windows that open.

Know your local building codes. Or hire a builder or architect who does. Usually city or county specifications govern windows.

Plan for the costs. Not only are large windows more expensive to order than smaller ones, installation is more expensive too, sometimes requiring more labor and equipment.

3

4

1 *Salvaged, rough-sawn boards and antique-style hardware give a barn-like feel to the cozy spaces under the eaves. The antique clock dial's huge size works with the room's lofty proportions.*

2 *A Palladian window provides ventilation and allows a flood of light to pour into the sitting room.*

3 *The hallway separates the sitting room from the bedroom; the door at the hall's end leads to the bath. Hand-painted pine flooring complements salvaged barn beams that frame the space. A black-and-red star painted on the floor underscores the color scheme in a bold way.*

4 *Each bed tucks into its own dormer in the bedroom, maximizing light, space, and privacy.*

Suite Attic
Retreats

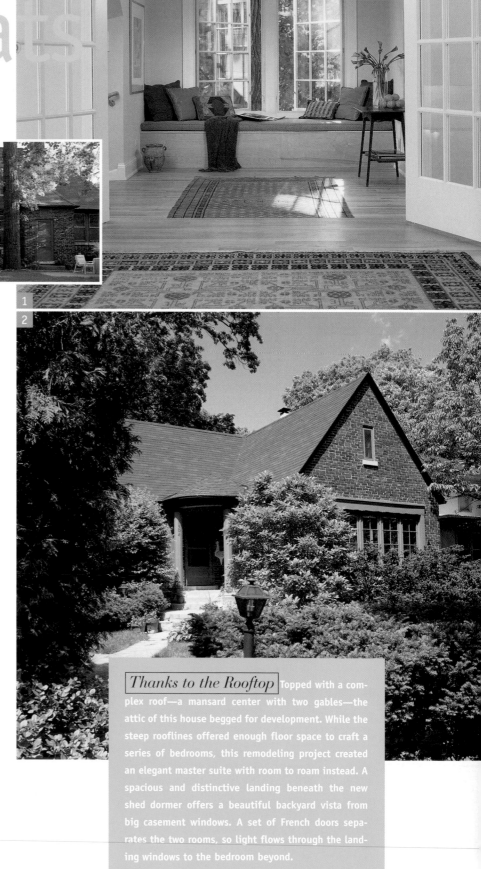

Case Studies If your roof is supported with open, A-frame-style rafters rather than zigzag trusses, your attic has the potential to become a lofty master suite. Check out the attics-turned-suites on these pages for inspiration. Whenever you convert an attic to living space, you have to meet your local building code headroom requirement—most likely 80 inches of height over 50 percent of the floor space. If you don't have that kind of space, there are solutions: You can raise collar ties or install window-fitted dormers that add headroom and floor space, plus light and architectural intrigue. And don't fret about fitting in a full-service bathroom: they fit in even the skinniest slivers of space. So draw a sketch of your attic, jot down some rough measurements, and head to your city's building and zoning department. Building officials will tell you what building codes you need to meet and become helpful partners in squeezing suite dreams from your upstairs space.

Thanks to the Rooftop Topped with a complex roof—a mansard center with two gables—the attic of this house begged for development. While the steep rooflines offered enough floor space to craft a series of bedrooms, this remodeling project created an elegant master suite with room to roam instead. A spacious and distinctive landing beneath the new shed dormer offers a beautiful backyard vista from big casement windows. A set of French doors separates the two rooms, so light flows through the landing windows to the bedroom beyond.

Dormer *Secrets*

Dormers—essentially raised roof areas that lift out of the main roof—fall into two categories. Shed dormers, like the one rising out of the brick home, *opposite page inset,* appear to have been cut and lifted up from the main roof. Gable dormers have rooflines that run perpendicular to that of the main roof (see the home exterior featured on page 50). Many houses feature a series of gable dormers that face front, with a shed dormer that lifts out to the back. By adding dormers you can discreetly add an entire floor to your home. If this remodeling project had simply added a full-walled second story to the house, the house would appear massive and out of place among its neighbors. Large or small, the best-looking dormers are built with windows that align with features above and below them.

4

5

1 From the landing's tall windows, light spills down the stairs to the left and into the bedroom in the fore-ground. The landing with its comfy bench feels like an extension of the bed-room and adds as much drama to the exterior of the house as it does inside.

2 The front of this 1929 brick Tudor gives no hint of the light-filled haven tucked beneath its steep roof.

3 Suite volume: At 1,190 square feet, an attic this large easily could have yielded two or three bedrooms.

4 Placed beneath a gable off the landing, this bath features dramatic angles and lots of geometry in the form of tiles and a mirror. A skylight opens views to the treetops.

5 In the bedroom, part of the roof was cut away to create a recessed window wall that faces a side yard. Built-ins to the left create a media center with plentiful storage and lots of display space.

Suite Rising A cavernous space existed above this Atlanta bungalow, but the owners simply didn't know how to get at it. The entry was small and oddly placed. An architect helped reconfigure a first-floor closet and bath, freeing up space so stairs to the attic could be piggybacked over existing stairs leading to the basement. This stairway solution provides easy access to a 300-square-foot bedroom, a 100-square-foot bath, two roomy closets, and an office.

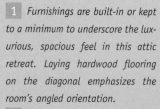

1 Furnishings are built-in or kept to a minimum to underscore the luxurious, spacious feel in this attic retreat. Laying hardwood flooring on the diagonal emphasizes the room's angled orientation.

2 This 1917 bungalow netted an almost 50-percent increase in square footage by wedging an office and master suite into the attic.

3 Replacing a hipped roof with a full gable at the back of the house created more headroom. The improved roofline also makes way for a bank of casement windows and a French door that opens onto a balcony, left.

4 The bedroom's angled wall positions the bed for a clear view to backyard scenery, as well as to a built-in media center outside the closet to the right of the bed.

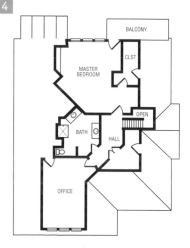

1 A gas fireplace divides the attic into two comfortable areas by lessening the tunnel-like feel of the space. The hall knee wall is fitted with stock cabinets for storage and provides access to the closet/dressing area, and stairs.

2 The raised roofline of an existing low dormer frees up headroom for a double vanity bath and two small casement windows.

3 A new to-the-peak boxed bay attic window adds character to the cottage exterior and floods the attic suite with morning light.

Space-Savvy Suite

The attic of this 1906 cottage has only 360 square feet of floor space, but smart, space-saving moves transformed it into a gem of a master suite. A soaring ceiling and to-the-peak windows give the space an expansive feel. Stairs were well-located from the start, but an old brick chimney was removed to permit the open floor plan. Placing the bath near the middle of the attic afforded easy access to the plumbing lines in a bath below. In the closet/dressing area, stock cabinets—an affordable alternative to built-ins—are snugged into a bump-out to serve as dressers. In the sleeping area the same cabinets tuck into a recess, creating a cozy nook and bedside storage as an alternative to a space-gobbling headboard.

Nontraditional Housing

One of the benefits of remodeling is that it allows you to choose all kinds of structures—not just houses—as your starting point. Here are three case studies of to-die-for houses that all started life as something else: a barn, a church, even a stonecutting factory.

Before

The world of real estate is full of great old buildings brimming with potential—and many of them are not houses. Don't let that stop you. If you're looking for a great piece of architecture in a particular location, broaden your perspective to include agricultural, commercial, and even industrial spaces. You may be surprised by how many diamonds in the rough you can find. And despite the creative demands and work they require, you may even land a bargain.

1 The exposed post-and-beam structure of a 1790s barn is overlaid with a tracery of windows in this conversion. The rustic floor is covered with planks that formerly were the barn's walls. Antiques lend sophistication to the simple interior.

2 Nearing collapse when it was found, this New Hampshire barn's frame was nevertheless sturdy and intact. Its pieces were numbered, dismantled, and trucked to a new site in Connecticut.

3 The barn was too long for the new lot, so its midsection was removed and repositioned at right angles to the main section. The midsection now serves as a garage and guest apartment.

Nontraditional buildings generally offer sturdy construction and an abundance of large, open spaces that you can configure to your liking. On the other hand you probably have to start from scratch when laying out everything from a residential floor plan to mechanicals, surface treatments, and landscaping. Plenty of

1. This Harbor Springs, Michigan, church was reborn as a residence. Its big, open spaces offered the new owner a blank canvas of possibilities. With a palette inspired by impressionist painters and detailing reminiscent of a French country barn, it serves as both a house and studio.

2. The restoration excavated the wood floor from beneath generations of sheet coverings. The second level was removed, allowing for a cathedral ceiling in much of the living area—the former sanctuary— and a sleeping loft, visible at the top of the photo.

Nontraditional Housing

time and the assistance of a sympathetic architect, contractor, and perhaps even an engineer, are key to successfully transforming these spaces.

Finally, make sure the building you're looking at can be modified for safe and healthy habitation and that the surrounding neighborhood is to your liking. Consult with an environmental engineer and local public health and safety officials to determine whether the site you are considering has known health or safety risks.

Before

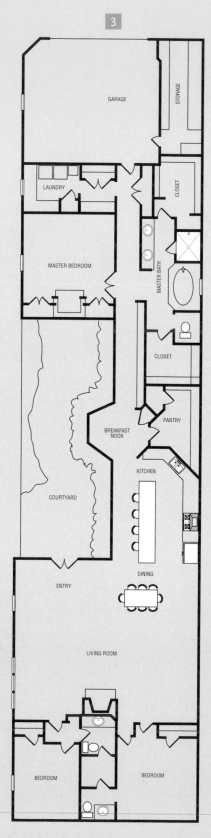

1 Factory doors that once opened for the delivery of enormous blocks of limestone were replaced by wrought-iron gates that lead to a courtyard. Restrictions mandated the preservation of the building's existing openings in the historic Germantown district of Columbus, Ohio.

2 French doors open to a patio, bringing some of the outdoors in.

3 The unusually long and lean floor plan affords lots of entertaining space indoors and out while providing privacy by separating the master suite from the guest rooms.

4 The building's 165-foot length necessitated a floor plan with a hall. To help distract from the hall's length, the project lined a portion of the corridor near the master bedroom with built-in bookshelves.

5 Cutting away a portion of the roof in the center of the house created a courtyard that floods the entire interior with both light and views.

Sometimes the only way to gain the space and functionality you need is to add on—either by bumping out or bumping up.

Within each of those two moves lies a spectrum of choices. Bumping out involves adding anything from a breakfast nook to a whole new wing. Bump-ups range from adding a family room above an attached garage to completely redesigning a ranch to get a twice-as-big, twice-as-tall two-story home.

Additions are a quantum leap in remodeling com-

plexity compared to working within your home's original exterior walls. Substantial additions often entail revamping the home's existing mechanical systems and some reworking of the home's original space, exterior detailing, and even its landscaping. Projects of this complexity are best tackled with the help of an architect, an interior designer, and a landscape designer.

The results, however, can be truly spectacular. And if you're loath to leave your friends, yard, neighborhood, and schools, the benefits of adding on instead of trading up are immeasurable.

Remodel

The Block Plan

Case Study This turn-of-the-century summer cottage on the Maine coast had such draw that it was renovated into a four-season home. Because full-time living requires a bit more room than vacation living, the project involved adding an entry, a larger kitchen, and a bath to the first floor and an art studio in a second-floor tower.

The project left the main house intact and added on in geometric pieces: an octagonal tower, a rectangular foyer, and a fan-shape kitchen. The block-by-block approach minimized the need for structural or design changes within the original cottage. And the octagonal and fan-shape exterior walls allow the house to capitalize on its coastal views more than ever before.

For houses within 75 feet of the mean high-water mark, Maine law restricts additions to 30 percent of the original square footage. In this project's case, the limit was 600 square feet, so an efficient use of space was key. Preserving the original cottage's Craftsman-style charm was a priority as well. The simple, geometric additions complement the original cottage's square shape.

Some invisible but important changes took place as well: The chimney was rebuilt to accommodate a furnace—the home's first. Insulation was added, and a radiant-floor heating system—chosen for its efficient warmth and lack of intruding registers or radiators—was installed. Finally, the house, which had been lightly built on a ledge, was firmly fastened to the ground with steel and concrete underpinnings.

1 The renovation bumped out the east wall of the house to create a foyer that links the new tower and kitchen to the old structure. In a salute to the sea, a compass adorns the entry and a boat hardware serves as a hat rack.

2 Shingles, gables, window styles, rooflines, and details such as exposed rafter tails help the new additions mimic the original structure.

3 Painted beaded-board paneling and clear-finished bird's-eye maple surrounds the whirlpool tub in the new bathroom. Windows afford a spectacular view of the cove below. Shelving just below the ceiling was custom-made to hold glassware found at flea markets.

4 A new stairway leads from the foyer to the tower room, the homeowner's art studio.

5 Replacing the typical over-sink medicine cabinet, a custom-made tile mural of plants and fish reinforces the room's ties to the water. A glass shower keeps the bathroom open and light.

Lighting *with Color*

Originally the brilliant coastal sunshine on the second floor was drabbed-down by plain fir floors painted a dull brown. The solution: Paint the walls white for maximum reflectivity, then liven up the relatively plain interiors with brilliantly painted floors. Hues of raspberry, lemon, orange, and mint now reflect as pastels on the white walls. High-gloss enamel floor paint allows the original floors to remain exposed and provides a durable, wipe-clean surface. The idea was such a success that ripples of color cascade down the main staircase.

63

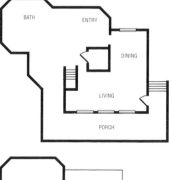

1 Fifteen windows provide a 360-degree view in the new tower, a perfect location for an art studio. The roomy window seat stores art supplies without hampering enjoyment of the sun and surf.

2 White, half-moon treads painted on the main staircase are both artful and practical, as they make the steps easier to see at night.

3 A luminous yellow floor brightens the otherwise dimly lit upstairs hall. Imperfections in the original fir floor "age down" what otherwise might seem a contemporary color treatment.

4 A mint-green floor adds vibrancy to the white-on-white scheme of a bedroom in the original cottage. Inspiration for the color palette came from the vividly hued wrappers of chewy candy.

5 The raspberry floor in this original bedroom throws a warm wash across the white walls and exposed beams.

A Room for All Seasons

Cupola on the Rooftop You may find a cupola now and then on an early colonial building, but they didn't really gain popularity until the mid-1800s when fanciful cupolas—some of them the size of full rooms—graced Gothic and Italianate Victorian houses in the United States. Cupolas can be designed to blend with the architecture of any style house and actually help cool a house during hot weather. With the cupola open and all but the first-floor windows shut, warm air wings its way up and out, pulling in cooler air behind. With a roof overhead, cupolas actually block summer's hot overhead sun, yet allow ambient light and winter daylight to enter.

1
2

Case Study This Long Island ranch was missing comfortable space in which to round up and enjoy family and friends. An addition was the solution, but it needed to satisfy a lot of contrasting desires: simple yet grand, large yet intimate, winter-cozy and summer-airy. The smart furniture arrangement in the new 26-foot-square gathering room meets the demands of a family that gets together often or enjoys entertaining. By placing lamps around the perimeter of the room—and wedging a pair between the sofas on a tall table—the room stays amply lit when the sun goes down. Everywhere you look, there's a cozy place to snuggle in for conversation or a nap.

1   *The boundaries between inside and out blend together beautifully with the help of French doors that open to an arbor-covered patio.*

2   *With blue-stained cedar shingles, white trim, and a mass of windows, the addition is in keeping with Long Island's shingle-style architecture. The arbor, in place prior to the addition, is now a wisteria-covered entry.*

3   *Big bay windows and a ceiling that vaults to a light-filled cupola make for a cheery mood throughout the gathering room. The beamed ceiling echoes that of the kitchen for a consistent feel between the original house and addition.*

4   *Back-to-back sofas form two cozy seating groups in the large room. One faces a focal wall of fireplace and bookshelves; the other looks out to the patio gardens.*

Ranch

Dressing

1 *Adding a second story requires inserting a stairway. Set in to dormers, the staircase and surrounding center of the home is bathed in light.*

2 *At the time of purchase, the home had not been improved since the '50s and was nearly buried in overgrown plantings that darkened the interior and obscured the view.*

3 *Same footprint, very different house: Interesting rooflines and dormer windows bring the outdoors in and allow for two additional bedrooms upstairs. A landscaped front yard makes for beautiful views from inside.*

4 *A barrel-vaulted entry adds interest to the facade, and light and drama to the interior.*

5 *Light pours into the new living room through dormers in a new, beaded-board cathedral ceiling. A white mantel and fireplace surround enhance the bright interior.*

6 *Dark paneling, a massive rock fireplace, an oppressively low ceiling, and lack of windows lent a cavelike feel to the original living room.*

7 *Slate countertops and warm maple cabinetry create a country look. Built-in corner hutches and the desk with a window view make the room multifunctional.*

Case Study A huge stock of 1950s ranch-style houses in this country are waiting to be rediscovered. While their ground-hugging profiles, rectangular shapes, and sometimes unimaginative, chopped-up floor plans may not be immediately attractive, many are situated on great pieces of property in desirable locations, making them worth a second look. As this case study shows, a custom-designed renovation works wonders to bring about an amazing transformation.

The ranch's one-story construction and simple lines make adding square footage and architectural interest an easier remodeling endeavor. You can double the size of a ranch without digging new foundations, giving up yard space, or having to run mechanicals over long distances. These advantages keep the costs of a major redo relatively low compared to adding the equivalent space to a multistory house.

In this case it was the home's location—in picturesque Rowayton, Connecticut, and on a pond—that sold the house. A dysfunctional floor plan of formal, cloistered rooms did not take advantage of the house's parklike setting. Nor did it encourage the kind of open, informal living and casual entertaining that the new homeowners envisioned.

The remodeling plans opened up almost the entire first floor, dissolving boundaries between the kitchen, entry, and living and dining rooms. The project eliminated one bedroom, added a laundry room, and retained a first-floor master suite. Building up from there, it added a second floor

with two bedrooms and a bath, allowing adult children to visit this empty nest and offering up some privacy while they're there.

Before

Beaded *Beauty*

Once relegated to lake homes, no-nonsense kitchens, or porch ceilings, beaded board is now the retro rage in all kinds of remodeling projects, thanks to its simple charm and surface texture.

Purists seek vintage stuff in architectural salvage shops, but easier, off-the-shelf alternatives abound. Solid pine or cedar plank beaded board offers design flexibility. These tongue-and-groove boards are installed vertically, horizontally, diagonally, or in a herringbone pattern. Traditional 4-inch widths with varying degrees of thickness are available, commonly in 8-foot lengths.

Beaded-board panels, available in 4×8-foot sheets or precut to 32-inch wainscot height, are available at home center stores. Some are offered with a prefinished veneer of a variety of species, including oak, maple, and birch; others are unfinished and ready to paint. For a primitive look or for outdoor applications, check out exterior-grade pine plywood, available in a sanded or rough-sawn surface.

1

Old Beams can give a new renovation instant charm—especially if you live in a vintage home. But they often are expensive and hard to come by.

Fortunately it's fairly easy to get an aged appearance from new, relatively inexpensive lumber, if you know what to ask for and how to treat it. Specify *green* (freshly cut, not fully dried), rough-sawn beams at your local lumberyard. Before installing them apply a dark stain, followed with a whitewash for the slightly mottled look of age. Unlike dried lumber, green wood cracks over time as it dries, giving it a naturally distressed look.

Staying
Home

Case Study If you love your house too much to leave it behind but you really need more space, consider adding on. Two additions helped this small Tudor starter home grow to match the changing needs of its owners. The first phase of the remodeling added two bedrooms and a bath above the dining room to accommodate growing children. A second phase added a 13×13-foot bump-out to the existing family room, which is located right next to the kitchen, for additional dining space. (The room now seats up to 16 people.) The addition boasts features that are as visually pleasing as they are functional—a cozy fireplace, a TV nook set into a fieldstone wall, and beamed ceilings. Although arched windows are new style element for this particular house, the shape is in keeping with Tudor-style homes of the same period as well as the roofline of the dormer.

The addition and remodel cost approximately $150,000, but thanks to a great location, the homeowners expect to recoup their entire investment—with interest—when they sell.

Before

After

Hiding *the TV*

TVs aren't the most attractive appliances when turned off, so many homeowners hide them in armoires or entertainment units. However, in a small room dominated by a fireplace, finding an appropriate spot for the TV can be difficult. Thanks to innovations in fireplace design, you can now have your fireplace and your TV. In the addition *below* the TV resides in a recess in the chimney. A metal flue runs behind the recess, so the television stays cool even when a fire is lit. Direct-vent gas fireplaces make this trick even simpler, as they vent directly to the rear of the firebox.

1 A large pass-through from the galley kitchen to the family room visually expands both rooms and is perfect for snacking and chatting.

2 The addition's scale, rooflines, and window detailing match the rest of the house.

3 Pigmented plaster and rough-sawn beams add cottage character to the dining room.

4 The family room addition features a cathedral ceiling covered with tongue-and-groove boards and a natural stone veneer fireplace wall. Arched doors over the firebox conceal the television.

Bungalow
Moves Up

Case Study Conventional real estate wisdom encourages prospective homeowners to "buy the worst house in the best neighborhood you can afford." Here's a corollary: Buy the smallest house in a neighborhood of multistory rowhouses, then build up.

Over many years, this early-20th-century brick bungalow found itself hemmed into the shadow of taller neighbors. Like a sapling in the understory of a forest, it seemed destined to wither and die.

Instead all the surrounding change created the precedent for a major renovation. The modern-style, glass-fronted buildup might have been out of place in a quiet suburb or quaint small town, but this sleek facade is right in step with the urban-chic feel of Chicago's Bucktown.

The primary goal was to increase the house's space and light while giving it a fresh, contemporary style. The renovation maintains the facade's original openings but fills them with the maximum amount of glass, including a frosted front door that allows light but preserves privacy. Adding a significant amount of glass does have a negative effect on energy efficiency, although added light and drama are well worth the cost. If you want vast expanses of glass, discuss the additional load on your heating and cooling with a qualified Heating, Ventilation, and Air Conditioning (HVAC) engineer to make sure your home's existing system can handle the new demand. Also consider high-tech glazing, which minimizes energy loss.

Interior walls came down, and the roof went up. Along with the soaring ceiling, a new curved cutaway and see-through elements give the interior an edgy, gallerylike feel. If you're considering alterations this bold, enlist the help of an architect or designer to make sure your plan both looks great and works well.

1 The rear of the house makes the most of space by locating a sun deck on top of a new garage. Cedar siding echoes the lines and tone of the decking.

2 No longer in the shadow of its neighbors, this former bungalow reaches for the sky with a glass-fronted bump-up.

3 A clever swoop of glass block wall separates the foyer from the living area without blocking the flow of light.

4 On the other side of the home, the family room breaks out of the box with a sinuous wall of windows. A built-in cabinet houses electronics; funky furnishings hold their own within the room's artful curves.

5 Contrasting floor coverings, a change in ceiling heights, and a two-sided fireplace denote a transition from the family room to this adjoining dining room.

6 This second-floor view shows how the addition's windows hug the original roofline. The end of the hall overlooks the family room below.

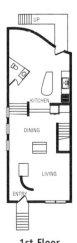

1st Floor   2nd Floor

Before

Work in
Progress

Case Study Occasionally a home is offered for sale midway through a renovation. Perhaps the homeowners ran out of money, time, enthusiasm—or simply moved to a new location before their dream could be realized. Whatever the case don't automatically dismiss someone else's unfinished project. You may be able to pick up a customized home that's well underway yet still offers you the chance to personalize the outcome.

On the other hand don't leap into a half-finished home without taking a good hard look. The project may have been ill-conceived from the start; unforeseen structural or other problems may have caused a previous owner to abort. Poor workmanship or shoddy materials—vain attempts to bring a runaway project back on budget—may compromise the result. At minimum, survey a potential buy with an architect, engineer, or contractor and have a firm idea of what's necessary to complete the work—or alter it to your liking—before making a bid.

This house began life as a one-story 1970s log cabin that was altered in the '80s with an unfinished second story and a nod toward Scandinavian style. It was, at best, a pastiche of dreams never completely realized. Contrary to the preceding sober advice, the new homeowner jumped to buy the place, charmed by its location on Bainbridge Island, a 30-minute ferry ride from Seattle.

Fortunately the largely unfinished interior gave the buyer a clear sense of the work needed to be done, a list that included little demolition. The project removed walls that

Before

1 A kit-built log cabin staked a claim on this great location in 1979 and provided a sturdy foundation for the renovations that followed.

2 No trace of the original 1979 log cabin is visible in the current exterior. An addition in the 1980s added a second floor and painted wood siding and trim.

3 A large fireplace would have overpowered the existing small living room and blocked light, so the project added a windowed niche as well as a cobble hearth.

4 Before the addition of the 6-foot fireplace niche, the living room was dark and cramped in spite of its white paint scheme.

5 The mantel is a Craftsman-style classic: a plain fir timber supported by corbels.

divided the kitchen from the dining room and turned two tiny bedrooms into a single, larger bunk room. Then the entire house was painted and trimmed simultaneously, lending a cohesive, refined rusticity to the home. Bump-outs at either end house a fireplace nook and a bay window.

Before 1st Floor

After, 2nd Floor

After, 1st Floor

1 Created by combining two tiny bedrooms, the bunk room serves as guest quarters and is furnished with nostalgic, personal pieces.

2 The addition of shelves turned this spacious upstairs landing and hallway into a library. Its best feature is a sweeping view of Puget Sound and the Olympic Range.

3 A separate flue at the exterior foot of the chimney forms an outdoor fireplace that warms guests while they enjoy quiet conversation or a match of over-size checkers on the patio/game board.

2
3

Pet Rocks Sometimes a single well-conceived focal point can pull disparate renovations together, and is worth the extra money. The centerpiece of this remodeling—and indeed of the entire house—is a rock fireplace and chimney. Inside, it sits like a gem in its own bump-out niche, Arts and Crafts-style. Outside, the 35-foot chimney scales the full height of the house, creating an artful backdrop to a side deck that ties the home to its island location. Six tons of glacier-tumbled rock was hand-picked for uniformity and color from a local quarry, then painstakingly assembled by a master mason over a six-week period. The $12,000 cost was worth every penny to the homeowner, who says the fireplace chimney is the focus of every gathering, inside or out.

1

Switching Styles

Before

Case Study Changing the look, as well as the function, of a house is what every remodeling project is about. With planning and forethought, the results can be astonishing. Take this example: A boxy-bland ranch becomes a full-blown Arts and Crafts redo that looks authentic enough to fool even practiced eyes.

This project offers several lessons on how to make a successful stylistic transformation:

First, start with a house that's a good base upon which to build. Look for one having several key elements that are congruent with the style you're aiming to achieve. In this remodeling project, the existing ranch featured the same long, low profile, generous overhangs, and shallow roof angles also prevalent in

the Arts and Crafts style. Not having to change those major structural features made the project much easier to achieve.

Next, do your research. Read up on the style you want to emulate. Find sources for appropriate materials and detailing, and consult with an architect and interior designer who know the style well and can help you achieve a satisfying result.

Finally, make the project comprehensive enough to effect lots of changes at once: Halfhearted conversions look amateurish and may decrease, rather than increase, a home's value. In this case new siding, windows, doors, trim, and landscaping create a believable and congruent facade. Interior detailing was similarly comprehensive.

Salvage Savvy If you're attempting to replicate an historic architectural style, nothing helps you do it more convincingly than salvage materials. Not only do old windows, doors, built-in furnishings, molding, and hardware have historically correct forms and dimensions, they also have the patina of age.

Looking for and recycling old materials can be loads of fun and needn't be more expensive than buying and installing new. The best approach is to start gathering materials you may need (from architectural salvage yards, teardowns, and flea markets) before you need them. Then show your architect, contractor, and designer what you've assembled. That way, they can design your finds into your project from the start, decreasing costs and using the salvage materials to best advantage. If you can't find what you're looking for, there are plenty of reproductions available.

1 Much of the footprint stayed the same, but this Arts and Crafts bungalow, complete with Mission-style fenestration and stone-pier columns, bears little resemblance to the plain ranch from which it grew.

2 The newly expanded dining room features French doors that lead to a small front yard patio.

3 This fireplace and mantel were reconstructed from salvaged materials. Many furnishings are flea market finds.

4 The staircase to the new second story does double duty as display and storage space. The stained-glass windows, used here as doors, and hardware are salvaged items.

A Ranch
Grows Up

Case Study An initial facelift and pool addition made this run-down Dallas ranch livable for a while—so much so that it succeeded as a pool-side bed-and-breakfast and its owner longed for private space. The only way to go was up when an 809-square foot addition that yields a master suite and sitting room was annexed. The creamy palette makes this long, narrow second-floor space feel sunkissed as a seashell, and the fireplace divides the room without blocking window light or views.

Before

1 Shutter-style windows that open inward, flowerbox balconies, and new arches over the first-floor porch suggest Mediterranean style.

2 A direct-vent, two-sided fireplace with a limestone surround subtly separates the sleeping and sitting area without blocking light. Direct-vent units offer a great combination of aesthetic possibilities, efficiency, safety, and ease of installation. Sky blue window frames open into the whitewashed decor.

3 Echoing the pattern of the window's divided panes, a door of sandblasted glass leads from bedroom to bath.

4 Adding a second story to this 18-foot-wide, lackluster ranch proved to be an easy, smart way to enlarge the house. A ground-level addition would have called for foundation work, a most expensive option.

5 The suite's spare, peaches-and-cream scheme is refreshing. Windows facing the front of the house feature shutters that open inward.

6 The walk-in closets, built over a portion of the garage at the street end of the house, create a sound buffer against street noise.

Factory-Built Additions

If you're in the market for a new addition, consider buying one from a factory. The addition to the farmhouse on this spread bears little resemblance to the "modular" homes of a decade ago.

As odd as that sounds, factory-built additions aren't only possible, they offer many advantages over on-site construction. Among the positives: lower cost, faster completion, and less disruption.

Here's how they work: An architect draws up a plan (modular construction can accommodate just about any design). The manufacturer breaks down the design into modules that can be transported to the site by truck, then builds the modules on an assembly line. Modules arrive complete with plumbing, wiring, ductwork, carpet, fixtures, and trim already installed. They are lowered into place by crane under the supervision of a local contractor, who also prepares the site, completes the hookups, and adds finishing touches.

Because of the factory's bulk buying power and assembly-line efficiency (there are no weather delays, subcontractor no-shows, or waiting for materials, for example) costs are often half as much as on-site construction. These days modular construction is every bit as sturdy as on-site—indeed, quality can be even better because materials are protected from weather during construction, and factory equipment allows for precise assembly.

Just as important is the speed and efficiency of the process: Modular homes typically take less than half the time it takes to build on-site homes. Building a major addition on-site often takes months and involves nearly complete disruption of the original living quarters. A modular addition, on the other hand, is ready to live in just days after arrival.

Where to Get Yours Modular-home manufacturers are located throughout the country. Pick one that's relatively close to your home to minimize transportation costs. For more information or the names of modular builders, contact the Modular Building Systems Council of the National Association of Home Builders at 800/368-5242, ext. 8576, or write 1201 15th Street, NW, Washington, DC 20005. You can also visit www.buildingsystems.org.

1

1 The simply furnished bedroom on the addition's second floor offers no clue to its assembly-line origins.

2 This sunny family room occupies much of the addition's main floor. It incorporates custom windows and an oak floor that were delivered to the factory, then blended into the final construction.

83

Put on a Sunroom

If your house seems particularly confining when temperatures drop or days grow short, break out by adding a sunroom. A window- or screen-lined addition gives you the opportunity to soak up sunshine and fresh air from every angle. Seek the advice of an architect or building pro; doing so helps you achieve a sunroom that blends with your home's architecture and boosts the value and aesthetics of your house. For inspiration look at the examples shown on the following pages.

Timber and Screens for a Tudor

Heavy timber framing and a limestone hearth and floor create a rugged screened-in porch that's a visual match for the stately Tudor architecture of this Minneapolis home. The homeowners in this case adore the outdoor feel and did not want windows between themselves, the sun, and cool Minnesota breezes. The lure of the fireplace—surrounded by comfortable, durable furnishings and free from bugs—is strong. This room off the kitchen gets used April through November.

1 *Nothing is flimsy about this screened-in sunroom. Its architectural detail matches the heft and strength of the house it's attached to. Limestone floors and gorgeous yet weather-hardy furnishings invite relaxed fireside conversations and stand up to the elements.*

2 *The porch floor extends beneath the screen framing to form a walkway. A wrought-iron railing, steps to a lower patio, and broad swaths of landscaping blend the porch into the sloping backyard.*

3 *Two timber pendants on each rafter tie add decorative detail and form a pathway to the limestone hearth.*

Before

Match Up Mass, Detail

A tall ceiling, and windows that nearly reach it, keep this gathering space filled with sunshine until dusk. The sunroom is the base of a three-story addition that opens a grand 1912 Arts and Crafts-style home to the outdoors. Roof, mass, and materials are the keys to making this sunny addition appear as if it's part of the original house (see Seamless Additions on page 123). The sunroom interior underscores the latter two of those keys: The hefty beamed ceiling, window positioning and arrangement, and trim match those of the original house.

1 *Removing the odd little porch off the kitchen made room for a 22×18-foot, three-story addition with a sunroom on the first floor.*
2 *By infusing the addition with the same trim, features, and proportions used in the original house—and adding masses of windows—the house gains a sunny, open room chock-full of old-time ambience.*

Put on a Sunroom

Deck and Tub-Topped Sunroom

Two features usually found on the same level—a sunroom and hot-tub deck—create a stacked addition in this white, brick-and-clapboard cottage. The 18×5-foot, 6-inch sunroom base fits the original home's scale perfectly. On the second floor, French doors off the master bedroom open to a hot-tub deck, which called for the beefing up of ceiling supports and extended plumbing lines. The sunroom/deck addition, part of a second-story bedroom remodeling job, required the widening and raising of an existing shed dormer's roofline. Over the deck a gabled arbor connects the space to the home's architecture.

1 *For an unfiltered shot of sunshine, the owners of this home need only roll out of bed and onto their hot-tub deck. French doors reveal its pretty arbor, creating a focal point for the room.*

2 *On the first floor, thoughtful details—including the bay window and peaked, lighted door detailing—shape what could have been a boxy addition.*

3 *The face of this cottage is like its neighbors'; nothing suggests the double-decker sunroom/deck behind it.*

1 Tile floors and pine paneling create a look that adapts to all four seasons. Strategically positioned track lights illuminate the room and highlight architectural features at night.

2 A gabled roof over the deck-turned-sunroom adds overall interest. Muntin grids, a Palladian-style transom, and angled corner windows emulate classic style.

Bring the Outside In

For budgetary reasons this glass-walled sitting/dining sunroom was built in several phases. First the owners framed the roof, carefully positioning its supports so windows, doors, and skylights could be added later. Next came walls of windows and doors, then skylights. A pair of operable skylights on each slope draws in sunshine and boosts air circulation. The room stays toasty all winter thanks to the home's gas-forced air system, a pair of electric in-the-wall heaters, and full-sun location.

Put on a Sunroom

Savvy Sunroom Pullout

A bright sunroom with a high ceiling topped the wish list of this saltbox's owners, but losing views from second-floor dormer windows definitely did not. The solution is a gable-roofed addition that joins the house by way of a low-roofed addition, leaving the pre-existing shed dormer intact.

1 *A band of divided light windows, and—on the peaked wall—a crownlike divided arch window, add shape and detail to the mass of glass.*

2 *The sunroom walls are taller than those on the adjoining home's first floor. Matching roof pitch keeps the addition in scale with the rest of the home. The tall walls provided a blank canvas for bands of transom windows and an arched gable window.*

Sleep Up, Sun Down

A screened porch project grew into a two-story 13×19-foot addition, yielding a sunroom and bedroom suite that looks like it's part of the original.

Sunny Side Up

A gracefully tiered window wall frames a sweep of sun-dappled lawn and towering oaks in this sunroom, an addition to a 1960s Connecticut ranch. Laminated wood beams cased in drywall dramatize the room's airy height. Beneath the finish materials, walls, and roof, foam-sandwich panels wrap the space in a blanket of superinsulation that tempers summer heat and winter chill.

1 The sunroom addition and its gabled roof reaches out to the woodsy landscape and shades the patio.

2 Lemon-hued walls suggest sunshine even when skies are overcast. Casement windows (to the side of the center windows) and the awning windows beneath them draw in fresh breezes. A bonus: The awning windows can be left open even during light-to-moderate rainfalls.

1 The sunroom's exterior sports wood trim boards for variety, while the bedroom's exterior matches the original house.

2 Wicker furnishings and a vintage floor lamp suggest old-world charm, but modern-day radiant floor heating keeps the slate floor toasty when the weather becomes cold.

Lofty
Ideas

Case Study Put a work-at-home couple in a 1970s ranch that's short on space and you'll find a gap that even a great location can't fill. The answer, in this case, is a second-story gabled loft addition. By building a loft instead of a full second story, the exterior mass of the house doesn't change and its scale stays in keeping with neighboring houses. The open loft provides ample office space from which to run a business—and room for a spacious art studio. In between, a comfy sitting area beckons visitors to kick back.

Yet another advantage of a loft is its connection to the first floor. Work-at-home parents can see and hear what's going on with the children's activities downstairs.

1 Following the roof pitch, a bank of fixed and casement windows creates an asymmetrical geometry that complements the gable's to-the-side position and the loft's modern look.

2 Open shelving and cabinets hug the walls, eliminating the need for lots of furnishings.

3 The gable's north-facing windows minimize glare on the computer screen.

4 Great paintings don't happen without a mess along the way. A 4×8-foot plastic laminate worktable and a sink in the corner make cleanup easy.

Classic Comfort
Beauty

Before

1

2

Case Study After 20 years of featuring only a miniature 4×6-foot bath on the second floor, this 1920s colonial house in Maryland got a major space boost by the addition of a roomy master bath. The new addition required something on the ground floor to support it—hence, the new library. Great care was taken to match the addition to the original house, including a review of 40 brick colors and custom-mixed mortar to match the existing material. When brick matches can't be found, contractors often recommend pulling existing brick from more minor structures, such as garages. If that's not possible, you can use complementary materials such as stone but keep trim details consistent with those of the original house.

Although the main floor rooms have 9-foot ceilings, the library is a full 2 feet taller, thanks to a couple of interior steps that take advantage of the sloping lot beneath it. French doors to the back of the library permit waves of light and views of the herb garden outside.

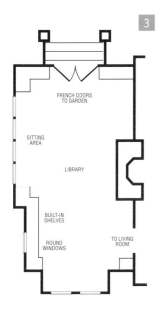

1 The two-story addition seamlessly attaches to the original house. Because it's fairly close to the sidewalk and could be imposing, the second level is stepped back and features decorative railing similar to that over the front door.

2 The herb garden just outside the French doors inspired the library's botanical motif and colors. The ceiling's slightly metallic ivy green color gives the room a luminous quality.

3 The first-floor library is a bonus that came with plans for the master suite on the second story.

4 Designed to hold books, collections, and a TV, built-in bookcases create a cozy feel for the seating areas and doorways. The round window in the middle is from the 1850s, a salvage piece collected years before building the addition.

Masterpiece Suite

Case Study Allow your passions to fuel your remodeling creativity. European country/Tuscan villa style drove the design concept in this new master bath suite. A love of world travel and the patina of old finishes inspires the casual use of furnishings and art—a theme echoed throughout the house. The new bathroom is in keeping with European hotel baths, measuring 18×15 feet with a cathedral ceiling that's 16 feet high at its peak. Furniture makes more sense than fitted cabinets in this space. A desk from the 1920s serves as a dressing table/vanity near the shower and tub. Chairs—part of a well-loved collection—find a place wherever a seat or landing spot for towels or toiletries is needed. Not visible (but important for protecting garments) is an exhaust fan in the dressing area.

1 Ocher walls and new floor tiles laid on the diagonal recall the style of European hotels. Collectibles such as furnishings and art add grandeur and a sense of place and history to the space. The glass surround of the shower is nearly invisible behind the antique soaking tub with its side-mounted faucet controls.

2 The second-story master bath replaced a tiny 4×6-foot bath—which is now a dedicated water closet. Note how the angled glass shower wall doesn't block the window.

3 Decidedly unfitted, this bathroom features twin pedestal sinks and an antique dresser that answers basic needs with old-world charm.

4 Open shelving between bedroom and bathing areas creates opportunities for storing necessities and displaying beloved objects.

Master Suite
Retreat

Case Study If you're going to place the bed diagonally in a room, why waste the wall space behind it? Based on furniture-arranging preferences, a diagonally placed wall actually creates more usable space in the bedroom, bath, and closet than a right-angled approach could. No unused corners or behind-the-headboard floor space resides in this 20×22-foot master suite addition. As a bonus, the diagonal interior wall maximizes views to the gardens outdoors; an array of pots and plantings are visible from the head of the bed. A walk-in closet sits just to one side of the bed, near the built-in dresser. Entry to the roomy master bath is between the bed and built-in desk.

PORCH

BATH

MASTER BEDROOM

CLOSET

1 Wall-hugging built-in furnishings and the diagonal wall make room for grand windows and window-like doors that lead outdoors and into the main house.

2 The 20×22-foot addition sidles half behind, half to the side of the house, creating a private porch entry and an intriguing footprint.

3 A built-in dresser and TV cabinet save floor space for foot traffic. Cherry stain warms the suite's white-on-white color scheme and echoes woodwork throughout the house. A divided-light door draws in sunshine and opens onto a private porch and garden views.

4 Thanks to the angled wall, there's plenty of room to snuggle into an oversize chair with a book. An ottoman serves as a second seating piece, footrest, or table. The trunk stores bedding inside and cups of tea and stacks of books on top. Windows on each wall of the suite frame garden views. Creamy tab-top window panels create a soft look and can be pulled for privacy.

5 To one side of the bed, a built-in desk hugs the wall and makes a prime spot for journal- or letter-writing while catching breezes off the porch.

More Attitude
Than Money

Case Study A squat lakeside cottage grew big, bold, and modern in a savvy remodeling project based on this sentiment: Use expensive materials judiciously and inexpensive materials lavishly. Topping the cottage with a second story and cantilevering a small addition left builders with no expensive foundation work to do. Inside, drywall and windows deliver loads of intrigue, lake views, and drama thanks to oversize geometric shapes and curves. To cut the cost of custom windows, most of the windows are fixed—only a select few are operable—and the owner/architect personally made the 1¾-inch window trim. Despite tight dimensions, no space here feels small, thanks to the open floor plan, pitched ceilings, and huge windows.

Second Story

Before you add another story to your home:
• Get a pro's advice. An architect or structural engineer can tell you whether or not your house can support the weight of a second story.
• Be prepared for extra work. Your existing walls and footings may need to be re-enforced, adding to costs.
• Consider the weather. Removing and replacing your roof is not something you want to do during the rainy season. Plan carefully to ensure that this stage is completed quickly.

1 Some wouldn't see the possibilities in this tiny, hip-roofed square of a Michigan lake cottage.

2 Stacking a second story right on top of the first was a budget-savvy way to double the size of the house. A two-story gabled entrance blends the two levels; an attached pergola creates a grand welcome.

3 The loft offers clear views of the lake. A glass railing—salvaged scrap from another remodeling job—offers safety and a sparkling view.

4 Interior views extend from the lakeside living room across the foyer and up to the second-story loft. Squares of scrap drywall add surface dimension to the wall where living room meets dining space; the squares also echo the cutouts in the master bedroom above.

If your home has a soul, it likely resides in the kitchen. The kitchen is the place to gather, recap the day, cook, laugh, and work. It can and should be a place for cultivating happy memories. A well-planned bath also can be one of your favorite rooms—a smartly appointed space that makes a luxury of getting ready for, or unwinding from, the day. But when these rooms fail to live up to your needs, your home becomes more of a frustration than a refuge. That's where good remodeling strategies come in. Take time to nail down exactly what isn't working in these rooms and become

informed about the options for making each space the best it can be. After you have a handle on the problems, look at the solutions posed on the following pages. The kitchen or bath of your dreams is closer than you might think.

Redo

Letting in Light

Case Study Contemplate ways to open up the kitchen to the rest of the house. This kitchen remodeling beautifully demonstrates what happens when the walls vanish—not only between rooms but also between the indoors and out.

For starters, the extrication of a wall between the kitchen and dining room expanded this kitchen from a U-shape plan to an island-focused galley that's ideal for gathering. The kitchen not only feels more spacious but also is open to sunlight coming into the new breakfast area.

The most dynamic turn, however, is the window wall that replaces a tiny window above the kitchen sink. Rather than flank the window with cabinetry, as would be typical, open cabinets hang directly in front of the window, allowing light to filter dramatically around the dishes.

While these ideas are contemporary, they didn't force the kitchen to sacrifice its farmhouse roots. Exposed rafters, beaded-board panels, a big, apron-fronted farm-style sink, and a reproduction faucet are just some of the features that preserve the vintage heritage.

Before

After

MUD ROOM

SITTING

KITCHEN

BREAKFAST/ DINING

1 A concrete island top is a rustic touch that suits the kitchen's old-fashioned look. Poured on-site, the countertops have 12 coats of concrete sealer to help the porous material resist stains.

2 Once an enclosed dining room, the new breakfast area joins the kitchen space to become one free-flowing room that's ideal for entertaining.

3 Light pours in through open cabinets mounted directly over a new window wall above the kitchen sink, dramatically backlighting an assortment of colored dishes. The large window also affords an expansive view of the yard.

4 One end of the island juts out like a table to create a comfortable workstation for food preparation or a place to sit and chat with the cook. Outside the work core a large green cabinet stores and displays collections and dishware.

Kitchen *Evaluation*

Traffic. Do kitchen entries impede the work core? Does the path to the refrigerator interrupt cooking? Does the table block entries?

Cooking. When preparing meals, are you cut off from others? Are there workstations for multiple cooks? Do you have ample counter space? Does your kitchen serve your cooking interests?

Cleanup. Is the dishwasher near the sink? How far is the table from the sink and dishwasher? Could you benefit from two dishwashers? Is there a place for recyclables?

Storage. Are your cabinets crowded? Would you like a walk-in pantry or a pantry cabinet? Are your existing refrigerator and freezer large enough?

Surfaces. Are the surfaces in good shape? Are they easy to clean and maintain? Is the flooring comfortable and attractive?

Light and views. Is your kitchen shadowy? How are views from the sink or range?

Dining. Do you have a place for dining in the kitchen? What seating difficulties do you encounter when you entertain?

4

Finesse a Floor Plan

For decades every efficient kitchen design was based on the *work triangle:* the triangular path from the center of the refrigerator to the center of the sink to the center of the range, with the total distance measuring no more than 26 feet.

The work triangle is still a good basis for gauging efficiency, but nowadays two-cook kitchens and task-specific workstations have many people tweaking the triangle to suit their needs.

Two standard workstations in a typical work core are the cooking area and the cleanup center. Equip your cooking area with the cooktop or range and microwave oven. A conventional oven that's separate from the cooktop is likely to be your least-

used appliance (unless you're big on baking) so you can place it outside the work triangle. Include ample countertops (at least 18 inches on each side of the cooktop) and storage for pots, pans, utensils, spices and seasonings, and other foods.

Design a cleanup center that has a sink, dishwasher, garbage disposal, storage for everyday dishes and utensils, as well as countertops on each side of the sink for food preparation and as a landing spot for dishware.

Some specialty workstations and their features are shown *opposite.* Ultimately the space you have available, the workstations you want, and the number of cooks who use the kitchen all influence your plan.

In addition to the galley configuration, shown in the photo *left,* four other basic floor plan options exist. Some are simply variations of a classic design with peninsulas and islands that serve as savvy modifiers. An island works well in a U-shape, L-shape, or single-wall kitchen because it shortens the distance between work centers and directs traffic outside the work core. Don't assume that islands have to be rectangular boxes of a standard height. They may run the gamut of geometric shapes with countertop heights varying. Similarly peninsulas don't have to be situated 90 degrees to adjacent cabinetry. Have fun creating your own design and allow your imagination to guide you while keeping the basic tenets of efficiency in mind.

1 Another view of the kitchen shown on pages 102 and 103 illustrates a variation on the galley plan. An island with range stands in as the opposing "wall" and routes traffic around the work core. Plan aisles at least 42 inches wide (or 48 inches for two cooks). For aisles without appliances, you can condense the space to as little as 36 inches.

2 An efficient work center combines two functions. Here a message center occupies the countertop with recycling bins below. The area could also function as a coffee center with bins below for pet food.

3 Set up a beverage area outside the work core so everyone can access glasses and the sink without getting in the cook's way. Consider substituting a small refrigerator or wine cooler for one of the lower cabinets.

4 Top a countertop with granite (the ideal surface for rolling out dough), and the beginnings of a bake center emerge. Cover the backsplash with pegboard to hang your most-used utensils in plain sight and within easy reach. Cabinetry within the station stores flour, sugar, and other baking needs. Locate the baking area near the ovens and close to the refrigerator for quick access to eggs, butter, and other cooled or frozen essentials.

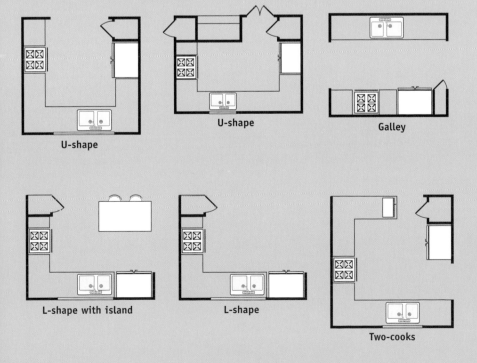

U-shape

U-shape

Galley

L-shape with island

L-shape

Two-cooks

Shaping Up **Your happiness in the kitchen has a lot to do with the shape it's in—literally. These basic kitchen shapes can help you form your work space. Remember, these are just guidelines.**

• **U-shape** *(with dual work triangles):* The U-shape configuration features a workstation on each of three walls and works best in moderately sized kitchens. Add an island to create multiple triangles in a large kitchen.

• **Classic L-shape:** In an open plan the classic L-shape places two workstations on one wall and the third on an adjacent wall. This arrangement works best when work flows from the refrigerator to the sink and to the cooktop.

• **L-shape with island:** You can modify the L-shape floor plan with an island, which is often used to divide the kitchen and family living areas.

• **Galley or corridor:** Ideal for small spaces, this arrangement allows the cook to move swiftly from one workstation to another.

Material Matters

Kitchen surfaces take a beating, so select materials that stand up to heavy use without losing their good looks. Here are some possibilities:

Counter Intelligence

Choose just one of these materials for your kitchen countertops or use two or more to customize work areas and attractively break up long surfaces. For example, you might want a stone slab for rolling out dough in the baking area or butcher block on the island. Install yet another material on the remaining perimeter cabinetry.

Stone, such as granite and limestone, is prized for its natural beauty and durability. Granite,

especially, can stand up to water, hot pots, and sharp knives. Regular waxing and polishing is necessary to maintain granite's luster. Marble and limestone are more porous than granite and therefore more susceptible to staining. Both must be frequently resealed.

Ceramic tile handles hot pans without scorching, is moisture-resistant, and comes in a host of colors, patterns, and textures. The tiles wipe clean with a damp cloth, though grout joints sometimes stain. To minimize discoloration install a tiled countertop using narrow grout joints and epoxy grout. Use scouring powder or household bleach to remove grout stains.

Solid surfacing comes in a variety of thicknesses and lower-cost veneers. A variety of colors, patterns, and look-alikes are available and the material is known for its design flexibility (for example, creating dimensional effects by using inlays of contrasting colors). Because the color runs through the material, nicks aren't so noticeable. The nonporous material resists stains but can be scratched or scorched. Minor damage, however, can be sanded out.

Stainless steel is popular for creating a commercial-style kitchen. It withstands the heat of pots and pans and is easy to clean. It will scratch, though, so it's not a good cutting surface. Choose finishes from a mirrorlike gleam to a matte glow; surfaces can be lightly brushed or highly relief-stamped or embossed. The shinier the surface, the more fingerprints and marks will show.

Butcher block brings warmth to a kitchen but requires periodic treatment with mineral oil. In spite of its name, butcher block is not suited for cutting meat because wood harbors bacteria. Use sandpaper to smooth out scratches.

Laminate is an affordable, low-maintenance surface that offers a tremendous range of colors, patterns, textures, and look-alikes. While laminate stands up to grease and stains and wipes clean with soap and water, it can't withstand knives or hot pans. Some laminates feature color through the material, making scratches and chips less visible.

Concrete works with a variety of styles, and you can have it colored or inlaid for custom looks. The material must be sealed regularly, though it's still subject to stains. It stands up well under heat.

Floor Show

Make your choice based on looks, easy maintenance, and comfort.

Ceramic tile comes in a variety of sizes and colors that allow you to create exciting patterns. The material is durable, resistant to moisture, and generally low-maintenance. But it feels cold, is unforgiving when you drop glassware, and is difficult to stand on for long. Food and dirt collect in the grout lines.

Laminate offers the look of wood and other materials at a lower price. Available in strips or tiles, laminate is durable, easy to clean, and requires little maintenance.

Vinyl is good-looking, inexpensive, and easy to care for. An enormous selection of colors and styles includes well-designed look-alikes. Available as sheets, tiles, and self-stick tiles, vinyl in tile form eventually loosens and admits moisture and dirt. Less-expensive grades puncture, fade, and discolor quickly.

Stone is elegant and nearly indestructible. Many types are low-maintenance. It is expensive, though, and is cold, hard, and unforgiving.

Hardwood lends warmth and a classic look to the kitchen. Although tough new finishes have made wood durable and maintenance-free, still it's susceptible to water damage in high-moisture areas.

Linoleum, which is made of primarily natural materials, is making a comeback. Soft underfoot, it comes in both tiles and sheets of solid or flecked colors and is easy to care for.

Cork provides a resilient, cushioned surface underfoot that is noiseless, comfortable, and moisture-

resistant. Made from renewable trees grown in the Mediterranean, cork requires a urethane finish to ensure easy sweeping and mopping. If you sand the old finish and reapply new urethane every few years, the flooring can last for decades.

Bamboo may look much like hardwood, but it's actually three layers of grass laminated under high pressure to create planks. Three coats of acrylic urethane render the surface durable and resistant to water, mildew, or insect damage. Harder than maple and oak, bamboo also expands and contracts less than hardwoods. And, unlike some exotic woods, bamboo is a renewable resource that's harvested after three and five years of growth.

Appliance *Points*

Some people want appliances to disappear; others want them to stand out. Manufacturers oblige both groups. You can integrate appliances into cabinetry with low-profile lines that don't show the controls. Panel fronts that match cabinetry, such as those on the refrigerator drawer *below right*, and radius-edge styling and curving corners help ease the transition from cabinetry to appliances. Beefy, bold appliances that mimic commercial styling address the opposite end of the spectrum. Stainless steel appliances always become a kitchen focal point.

A host of appliance innovations, such as halogen and magnetic-induction heating elements, convection/microwave oven combinations, and sealed-combustion gas burners (that guard against damage from spills), and features, such as high-output burners borrowed from commercial-grade appliances, mean faster cooking and easier cleanup. Other features include trimless knobs, touch controls, sleek, trimless dishwasher fronts; and smooth-top ranges with double ovens *below*. Sealed and raised edges on glass shelves in the refrigerator keep spills from spreading.

Well-appointed kitchens include such luxuries as an icemaker, compactor, wine cooler *below center,* and warming drawers *below left*.

Cabinet Criteria

While it's reasonably easy to pinpoint a look you love in cabinetry, beauty is more than skin deep. A basic knowledge of cabinetry anatomy—as well as which features signal quality—help you buy wisely. Here's a rundown of the basics:

Construction

Two prevalent types of cabinetry construction exist—face-frame and frameless. Face-frame construction features framing that is obvious to the eye, as it is attached to the front of the cabinet box. Drawers and pull-outs must fit within the framing, making these features slightly smaller than the overall cabinet width.

A frameless construction is marked by door hinges attached directly to the inside of the sides of the cabinet. The usable cabinet interior is slightly larger than that of face-frame cabinets.

Now take a closer look at the cabinet boxes. The sides, back, and floor of cabinet boxes are constructed of veneer-covered plywood, particleboard, or medium-density fiberboard. The sturdiest boxes are put together with dado joints, in which the sides fit into grooves cut into the cabinet back and face frame. (Boxes that are simply butted and glued are less sturdy.)

Triangular braces, called gussets, glued into the upper corners of the cabinet boxes, are positive signs of strength.

Pull out drawers next. Do they glide smoothly? If you pull out the drawer 1 inch and it closes on its own, it's equipped with self-closing guides—another desirable feature. If you can fully extend the drawers, you have full access to the inside without removing it from the cabi-

1 Cabinetry makes a dramatic statement in your kitchen. These cabinets sport fiery red stain—inspired by Ducati motorcycles—that give this loft kitchen a revved up, high-octane charge.

2 The hardware was custom-fabricated from an assortment of parts found at a home center store—turnbuckles, clevis pins, washers, and posts.

net. Good quality drawers feature dovetail or dowel joints at the corners, ½- or ¾-inch solid-wood sides, and plywood bottom panels glued into grooves.

Up Front

Doors and drawers fit the front of the cabinet in one of three ways:

Full-inset are flush with the cabinet frame. They require excellent craftsmanship and are available only on custom cabinets.

Partial-overlay conceals the opening but reveals some of the frame. This style is affordable because it's easier to construct.

Full-overlay doors are the only option available on frameless cabinetry because they cover the entire box front. Used on face-frame cabinetry, a full-overlay covers the entire cabinet frame.

Doors to Style

All cabinetry doors fit into two categories—frame-and-panel or slab construction. For frame-and-panel doors, a panel "floats" within the wood frame, allowing the wood to shrink and expand. Today the solid wood or veneered panel is often swapped for clear or patterned glass—allowing an entire or partial look inside the cabinet.

Solid-wood slab doors are more often found on custom cabinetry and consist of several pieces of wood that have been glued together to create the appearance of one solid panel. Wood crosspieces are screwed to the back for stability.

Shelf Expression

To avoid sagging, the best shelves are made from ¾-inch high-grade particleboard. Like the interior of the cabinet box, shelves are covered with a durable material such as laminate or melamine. Adjustable shelves are held in place with removable metal pins or plastic clips inserted into pre-bored holes.

For added convenience, roll-out trays—a cross between a drawer and a shelf—are becoming more common as standard features. They make better use of space than a shallow shelf, and the low sides provide easy access. Often subjected to as much or more weight than drawers, roll-out trays require the same high-quality glides as drawers.

Storage *Strategies*

Manufacturers offer recycling bins, drawer dividers, spice inserts, bread savers, pasta bins, wine racks, appliance garages, file drawers, and a number of other kitchen storage solutions. Ask your kitchen designer or cabinet salesperson to show you what is available with each line of cabinetry.

Keep in mind that corner cabinets make it difficult for you to get anything in the back without emptying the cupboard. Good solutions include lazy Susans and three-quarter-moon-shape shelves attached to the inside of the door.

Try these ideas on for size:

1) The location of drawers is just as important as capacity. These wide roll-out trays are near the dishwasher and at counter height to ease the task of putting away stacks of dishes.

2) Island shelves store more when outfitted with attractive baskets. The shelves are ideal for corralling produce, breads, and linens.

3) A sliver of space on each side of a cooktop holds single rows of seasonings in a slim-line roll-out spice rack.

4) This efficient pantry cabinet features pullout shelves and in-the-door storage. The rolling step stool puts top-shelf items within easy reach.

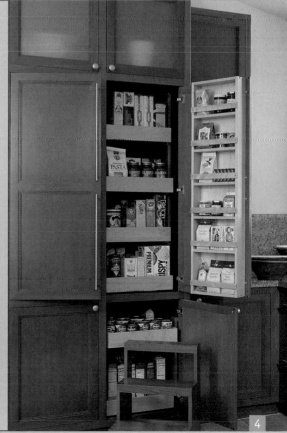

Capturing Comfort

Case Study If your dream is to create a welcoming haven in the form of a serene sun-drenched bathroom, let this renovation inspire you. It began as a 1980s-style room with a black toilet, a sunken tub, and tiny windows that were too high to see through. But dark and dismal transformed to light and cheerful, proving that there's hope

for most any bath. The remodeling wish list for this project included a roomy shower, a deep tub, double sinks, plenty of counter space and storage, and even a cozy chair. Windows, top to bottom, were also a high priority.

For starters a sizable addition pushed beyond the boundaries of the original 9×14-foot bath, allowing for

a roomy shower at one end of the room. Relocating a doorway to the opposite end of one wall created a niche for the toilet and enough room for a long vanity with dual sinks. On the opposite wall, three floor-to-ceiling windows replace standard-size windows. A new claw-foot tub basks in the natural light that now floods the room.

1 A claw-foot bathtub serves as the striking centerpiece of the bath. Tall windows keep it in the spotlight. Roman shades, installed just below the ceiling line, give the windows the appearance of being even taller than they are.

2 The walk-in shower's frameless glass door retains the open look of the bathroom while allowing natural light into the shower interior.

3 Relocating the doorway to the far corner left enough uninterrupted wall space for this extra-long vanity, topped with unfilled travertine. The base of the vanity echoes that of an antique French cupboard; the crackle-glaze finish enhances the classic look.

Make a Splash

Making thoughtful choices for your bathroom's layout, materials, and components help you shape an environment that's beautiful, relaxing, and easy to clean—whether it's a spacious master bathroom, a family bath designed to cater to kids, or a secluded powder room.

As you determine your basic needs—such as whether you want a separate shower and tub or if you need one sink or two—allow ample elbowroom around every fixture. List items you want to store in the bath, too, and where those items would best be located.

Consider where you'd like to place windows, and whether you want access to the outdoors. If privacy is a concern, plan a walled court-yard beyond the window or investi-gate glass block and translucent glass products to use instead of windows.

When choosing floors, counter-tops, and wall surfaces, look for quality products that stand up to high humidity and activity while meeting your decorative desires.

Countertops. Most countertop materials that are suitable for the kitchen (see page 106) also work in the bathroom. Although wood isn't a good choice for a heavily used bath-room, a well-sealed wood countertop brings welcoming warmth to a pow-der room or guest bath.

Walls. Glass and ceramic tiles, tum-bled marble, solid surfacing, and vinyl wallcovering add more than beauty to the bath. They're also easy-to-clean and far more moisture-resistant than plain drywall. Make your selection based on practicality, price, and the special look you want to create.

Floors. Many materials work well on bathroom floors, but ceramic tiles

and stone rank highest with many homeowners. For safety be sure to choose nonslip textured or matte finishes. Mosaic tiles also provide a great look along with a good grip underfoot, thanks to the abundance of grout joints. Some look-alike laminates are designed for use in the bathroom; ask a dealer which prod-

ucts are suitable. If you've decided on an authentic wood floor for the bathroom, choose one with a tough finish and make sure it's well-sealed after installation.

Tubs. When selecting a bathtub you'll find a variety of sizes, shapes, and functions. As you come across models you like, don't be shy about climbing in and testing them for a good fit and comfort. Keep in mind that a large water-filled whirlpool tub imposes substantial weight on floors. Locating a tub near an outside wall or perpendicular to floor joists aids in carrying the load. Have an engineer or architect help you determine whether floor joists beneath the tub require beefing up.

Faucets. Check proportions, handles, and finishes (make sure the manufacturer guarantees lifetime protection from scratching, tarnish, and corrosion). Ceramic disk valves are unaffected by temperature extremes and hard water, which means less chance of a leaky faucet. You also may want to consider a faucet that pulls out and doubles as a spray; other models operate on a sensor that allows no-hands operation.

Antiscald devices. Protect yourself and family from hot-water burns with safety devices installed at the faucet. Adjustable safety stops restrict how far the handle can be pushed toward "hot." Pressure-balance valves, most commonly found in showers, protect users from drastic temperature changes when other water-using appliances are turned on. Thermostatic valves maintain a preselected, safe temperature.

Sinks. Round, oval, square, rectangular, undermount—even bowls installed on top of the counter—are just a few of the sink options available. Porcelain is standard, but you also can find sinks that are hand-painted or fashioned from glass, stone, and various metals. Some glass sinks are lighted from below to emit a soft, pleasing glow at night. While all of these materials are durable, stone, porcelain, or glass are easiest to clean, so consider those materials for frequently used sinks. You may find water spots on metals bothersome. For fewer splashes on the countertop or floor, choose a deeper bowl. Locate the sink high enough to minimize stooping as you wash your face or brush your teeth.

Toilets. Even toilets come in myriad styles, shapes, and sizes. Some models are low-profile. Others hang from the wall (cleaning beneath them is easy because no skirt extends to the floor). Others feature heated seats and bidetlike fittings that offer a warm-water spray. Some even lower seats or flush automatically.

1 Wall faucets and raised sink bowls give this vanity a period look. The tablelike cabinet creates a library feel. Drawers and wicker baskets provide attractive storage.

2 Tranquil as an oceanside retreat, this bathroom owes its glow to sleek blue-glass wall tiles. Rough concrete stucco upper walls provide a dramatic counterpoint, while the smooth French gray limestone offers a comfortable surface upon which to perch.

3 Genuine tumbled marble countertop tiles provide an elegant foil for the oil-rubbed bronze faucet. The drop-in cast-stone sink matches perfectly.

4 Mosaic marble floor tiles, laid in a timeless wave pattern, form a border around white marble tiles laid on the diagonal.

The Well-Appointed Bath

Expand your thinking beyond toilet paper and towels to a bath that's a luxurious retreat. Don't be afraid to dream a little and think of ways to create a spalike experience in your own home. Then as you figure the budget and actual costs for amenities, do some horse-trading to gain the features you want most. Many of these little extras require a small investment but they will reap restful rewards.

Warm floor. Treat your toes to a toasty experience with a radiant heat system installed beneath the floor. Such a system is especially welcome beneath typically cold materials such as ceramic tile and stone. Add a layer of fashion and comfort with a gorgeous, soft area rug to plant your feet on when you step out of the tub or shower.

Comfortable seating. Whether you want a spot to sit down and towel off or just lean back and meditate for a few moments, a cushioned chair or ottoman ups the comfort quotient of any bath. Another option

is to place a cushioned bench beneath a window. Be sure to add lots of pillows.

Heated towel bars. Yet another cozy idea: Hang your towels from heated bars so you can wrap your entire body in warm terry cloth when you finish with your shower or bath.

Large tub. If you're longing to linger in the soothing jets and serene bubbles of a whirlpool tub, buy a model that's roomy and doesn't strain your back when you lean back. Keep in mind that you need plenty of hot water to fill the tub, which add to both your water and electric bills.

Luxury shower. Dual shower-heads, handheld pulsators, body sprays, and a broad bench—these are just a few of the features that make an ordinary shower lavish.

Soothing sounds. Whether you invest in a state-of-the-art sound system or stash a mini-CD player/radio on the shelf, keep your favorite soft music on hand for easy listening while you rejuvenate.

Television. To keep up with the news while you get ready for work, consider including a small TV in your remodeling plans.

A glowing hearth. Imagine enjoying the warmth of a fire as you relax in the tub or do your evening stretching exercises. Now make it a reality!

1 *Sometimes you need to plan very carefully to fit in all the amenities you're longing for. This extra-long bath, which measures 21×6 feet, features a tub cleverly placed in front of the window and an even larger shower in front of the tub. A clear glass shower wall and a door let light travel unhindered throughout the space.*

2 *Suspend a towel warmer on the wall; or take a cue from this bathroom and hang one on the side of the vanity.*

3 *Shapely new showerheads promise everything from drenching downpours to soothing sprays. Handheld showerheads offer convenience, control, and a range of spray sensations.*

4 *Create a cozy spot for morning coffee with a shapely upholstered chair that's nestled in a corner beside a sunny window.*

Walk-in Showers feel less confining, require less maintenance, and are easier to navigate for those who have difficulties with steps or thresholds.

• It's best to build an extra-wide shower to help keep water within the shower's borders. You still will likely need to protect more wall surface than you would with a conventional shower stall. Handle splashes by extending the waterproof surface of your showering area.

• Position the showerhead off-center and closer to a corner. A small lip in the floor at the shower's entrance helps contain water but may make the shower less accessible.

If you don't have sufficient space for a doorless shower or are worried that your room may be too drafty, consider purchasing a frameless door with minimal hardware and a lack of metal tracks; these shower doors seem to disappear.

Problem Solvers

Before

Bring In the Light

Problem: You're sleuthing for adjacent space to make your existing bathroom bigger, but you're still worried the space will seem dark and confining.

Solution: Pushing a window-rich 19-foot-wide addition outward and upward brings an abundance of sunlight and views into this bathroom. It also offers a nook for the whirlpool tub and two wings: one for an extra-large walk-in shower, another for a water closet. In the original portion of the bath, two vanities occupy opposite walls.

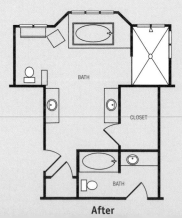

After

Privacy for Two

Problem: You both get ready at the same time every morning. While you love to chat, you don't necessarily want to watch each other brush teeth.

Solution: A long two-sided vanity with a mirror between the sinks provides visual privacy without blocking communication. Take a closer look—the mirror panel is only 2 feet wide; the rest of the frame is open. Situated in the center of the room, this vanity configuration allows for additional storage or grooming areas along the opposite walls. Beside the walk-in shower, there's also a separate compartment for the toilet.

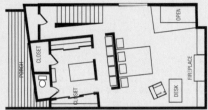

Gain a Laundry

Problem: You're tired of walking up and down the stairs to the basement to do laundry. Is it possible to find a place for the washer and dryer closer to the bedrooms?

Solution: Planning a large closet at one end of this bathroom, close to the entrance, offers the ideal location for a stacked washer and dryer that hides behind double doors when not in use.

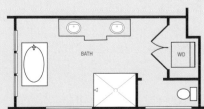

Now that you know the options you have for making your home more comfortable and beautiful, this chapter offers some additional insight to help you launch your dream.

First, you need to hire the best design and contracting professionals you can find, determine the building codes in your community, and establish what part your budget plays within the context of your home improvement project.

It also helps to understand the steps and phases of your project, how to make changes and additions appear seamless, and how to make sure the new floor plan flows with the rest of the house.

No matter how large or small your project, consider whether you can weave into your plans one of those optimal organizational spaces, such as a great mudroom or spacious closet.

After you've digested this chapter, ask yourself: Is remodeling truly the answer for me? If the answer is yes, review the tips on surviving a remodeling project—and you'll find yourself enjoying the journey as much as the destination.

The strategies that follow help you begin your remodeling adventure on the right foot so your home can become the best that it can be.

Restrategize

Selecting a Pro

Choosing the best professionals to design and build your remodeling project makes your entire experience more enjoyable and ensures top-notch results.

Whether you're searching for an architect or a contractor, use these tactics to track down the best one for you:

Gather. You need to collect names of professionals to investigate and interview. Ask friends and colleagues for suggestions and recommendations. Identify local referrals with the help of professional organizations, such as the American Institute of Architects (AIA) (800/242-3837, www.aia.org) or the National Association of Home Builders Remodelers Council (NAHB) (800/368-5242 Ext. 8216, www.nahb.com).

Explore. Call the architects and contractors on your list—you should have at least 4 to 6 from each profession—and ask for references. Then contact the people they name and ask them to recount their positive and negative experiences. Also, if you see a recent remodeling project that you like, contact the homeowners and ask about their experience and results.

Evaluate. Based on these references, interview the top three professionals who make the cut and tour some of their finished projects. Savvy architects and contractors will ask you questions as well to determine your expectations and needs. You should come away from each interview and tour with an idea of the quality of their work and how well your personalities and visions for the project match.

Solicit. To narrow your choices to between two or more architects, it may be worth the additional cost to solicit preliminary drawings from

In a desirable neighborhood of one-story ranches, this two-story transformation may start a trend. A gable, shallow roof pitch, and a blend of exterior materials keep the scale of this house in sync with its neighbors.

each one. This is a great way to test your working relationship. In the same vein, ask contractors for bids. Don't base your decision on cost alone. Instead weigh what you learned in the interview with the thoroughness of the bid itself.

Sign up. Before beginning a project with any professional, have the facts on paper to legally protect you before, during, and after the work is done. Define the scope of the project and fees as specifically as possible. The contract should include a clear description of the work to be done, materials that will be required, and who will supply them. It should spell out commencement and completion dates and any provisions relating to timeliness. It also should include your total costs (subject to additions and deductions by a written change order only). Payments should be tied to work stages; be wary of any contractor who wants a lot of money up front. If certain materials need to be ordered weeks in advance (to allow for manufacturing), then get a list of all those materials and their costs before committing to the idea of up-front money and making a down payment. Kitchens usually require a sizable cash advance to finance appliances and cabinetry.

Living within the Law

Your remodeling plans must be within the confines of the law, otherwise you may be required to make costly modifications.

Before you start any remodeling project, check your local building codes and ordinances. Most cities, towns, and municipalities have rules that determine where and what you can build. Although several kinds of local ordinances cover various

Zoning Variances To keep up with both technology and the changing needs of a community, zoning regulations are modified periodically. Therefore, if you live in an older neighborhood, your home may not be consistent with the zone in which you live. For example, you may have a single-family home in a commercial or multifamily zone. This is known as pre-existing, nonconforming use. In this instance any addition to your home requires approval from the municipality in which you live. This approval, called a variance, permits an exception to the rules for your specific situation. In some municipalities, achieving approval for a variance is a lengthy and difficult process. You may need to enlist the help of an attorney.

aspects of the remodeling process, the most important are zoning regulations, setbacks, and easements.

Zoning. These restrictions typically affect additions. If you are finishing your basement, for example, zoning may not be an issue.

Zoning regulations are designed to separate land uses to achieve the best use without interference from adjacent uses. For example, most municipalities won't allow a junkyard business in the middle of a residential area.

Zoning regulations cover four basic building issues: *height and width* rules denote the maximum allowable height and width of a structure; *use* rules specify its allowable uses, which include residential, commercial, industrial, and home-office considerations; and *density* rules specify the number of building units allowed per acre. Height and width are the two zoning restrictions that affect additions.

If you want to operate a home-based business, use considerations may affect you. But in all cases it's better to be safe than sorry, so it's a good idea to meet at least briefly with your local building code officials to see if you need a building permit to do what you're planning to do and to make sure your project won't violate any zoning restrictions.

Setbacks. Setback requirements mandate the number of feet between the building area and the property line. Setbacks are designed to pro-

vide adequate space between buildings for light, ventilation, access, and privacy. Most residential areas require 10 or more feet from the side property boundary to the buildable area. Setbacks for the front and rear are usually greater and depend on the size of the lot.

The best way to check your setback restrictions is to review your home's survey plat. If you do not have a copy, request one from your local municipal authority. To protect yourself from costly changes, do not build outside of your property's approved buildable area. If you do, even if you obtain a variance permit, both current and future owners of neighboring properties can force you to move your addition.

Easements. An easement is a legal interest in a parcel of land held by someone other than the landowner. The homeowner does not own the rights to the land use on an easement, even though it is on his or her property. For example, utility companies most likely have easements on your property, so they can run sewer or power lines where needed. You are not allowed to place any permanent structures on most easement areas. In some instances sheds or fences are allowed. It is highly unlikely that an easement can be changed to accommodate an addition, particularly if pipes or wires are located underground.

Stages, Phases, and Budgets

The center portion of this gable's new Palladian window matches the smaller arched window that is part of the original house.

Regardless of what area of your home you remodel, prepare yourself by knowing what to expect during the process and how to save money.

Most remodeling projects naturally divide into stages, or phases, whether you're remodeling a whole house or just the kitchen. Budget determines what can be accomplished during any particular phase—especially if you are remodeling on a pay-as-you-go basis.

While no two remodeling projects are exactly the same, they normally follow a process similar to the following steps:

1) Plan. During this stage you determine whether you're using a design professional. Whether you are or not, you need to pin down the design and begin shaping the budget. Next select a contractor, who may suggest alternatives for accomplishing some aspects of the design. During this stage, you also finish the budget, select many of the products for the project, and determine a timeline. If your contractor is using a job-site supervisor, you should meet this person and establish rapport.

2) Confer. Invite the key players to your home—the architect or designer, the contractor, primary subcontractors, and the job supervisor. Use this meeting to tour your home together and review the project particulars. This meeting, which could take a couple of hours or more, is also a good time to establish any ground rules between you and the professionals you hire. You especially need a good plan for communication. One option is to place a notebook in a prominent location. This is where both you and the crew can jot down comments and questions.

Check the notebook each day. Also, plan a weekly review meeting between you, the contractor, and the supervisor. Especially if you keep a detailed notebook, these meetings may be quite brief—from a few minutes to half an hour or so.

3) Prepare. Remove your personal belongings from the job site. The supervisor may come in with a trash bin, a portable toilet, and other equipment. To prevent dust and debris from spreading throughout the house, hang plastic sheeting and seal it securely between the job site and the rest of the house. During the course of the project, check the sheeting periodically for gaps and leaks.

4) Demolish. Any built-in structures, such as cabinetry, counters, islands, or walls that will not be included in the final project, are removed during this stage. Doing the demolition yourself may save you money. If that's an option you'd like to explore, discuss your participation with your contractor during the Plan and Confer stages.

5) Construct. If you're building an addition, the foundation and framing go up first with windows to follow. After that comes the plumbing, electrical wiring, and Heating, Ventilation, and Air Conditioning (HVAC) ductwork. Insulation, drywall, roofing, and siding are installed next. Finish carpentry and electrical connections follow, then the flooring. After that, appliances, light fixtures and plumbing fixtures are installed.

Wood floors can be sanded, stained, and sealed at this stage.

6) **Finish.** Walk through the completed project with your contractor and architect, noting any concerns or unfinished details. The contractor follows up on your list in order to complete the project.

Seamless Additions

The key to a successful addition is to make it look as though it has always been a part of the home. Details make a major difference.

To make your addition appear seamless, pay attention to three crucial factors: roofline, proportion, and materials.

Start at the top. Nothing announces a bad addition louder than a roof that doesn't match the one on the existing house. Whether gable, hipped, shed, or mansard, make sure all roof portions mirror one another in style. Matching the pitch, or steepness of the roof, also matters because it lends consistency to the overall image of the home. Overhangs, soffits, fasciae, and eaves all need to look the same.

Maintain proportion. Proportion, or massing, refers to arranging the main components of a house in relation to each other. When planning a renovation, take care that an addition won't overwhelm—or be overwhelmed by—the existing structure. When adding a second story to a 1950s ranch, for example, make sure there is enough mass on the second floor to balance the strong horizontal lines of the original home.

Choose materials carefully. The final key to making sure that your new addition doesn't look like an afterthought is uniformity in materials—from the roof on down.

This is easier said than done. When using brick, for example, its color, size, texture, and mortar all need to match the original exactly. If you can't find or afford to make a perfect match, your next option is to complement the existing materials with something consistent with the period of the house. If you have a Cape Cod-style house, for example, and don't want to spring for the hand-split cedar shakes used on the original part of the house, you'd be perfectly justified in choosing lap siding that's painted to match. Stained vertical cedar siding, on the other hand, perfect for many contemporary-style homes, looks glaringly out of place on a Cape Cod.

On the roof, match shingle style, color, and material. If circumstances prevent exact matching, select compatible materials, or better yet, replace the shingles on the existing structure at the same time you add them to the new one.

Windows, too, need to match. Coordinate the basic type (casement, awning, double-hung, etc.) and the details, such as the width of the mullions (vertical stripes that divide the panes) and the muntins (strips of wood or metal that adorn the panes) as shown on the seamless addition, *opposite*. Last, don't forget about color. Paint both the new and existing structures in colors that are appropriate for the style and the period of your home's exterior design. Explore your home's surroundings for color inspiration. You don't need to select colors identical to neighboring homes; instead, choose a color palette that is in keeping with its surroundings.

| *Controlling Costs* | If your plans and projects are bigger than your billfold, use these tips to help you save dollars: |

• Choose materials wisely. For example, birch cabinets cost two to three times less than solid cherry and can be personalized with stains, paint, or stenciling. You also can buy stock cabinets and customize them with molding.

• Get help. Swap jobs with handy neighbors. Throw a theme party and feed guests. Ask family and friends to help out.

• Assist as a general laborer. Consider doing simple grading, tearing up carpet, wallpapering, painting, and minor trim work and cleanup. A cost-plus-fixed-fee contract credits your labor against a contractor's fee.

• Act as your own general contractor. This is a full-time job, though, and not a task for the fainthearted. You need to understand the project, the order of work, and have a thorough knowledge of building codes.

• Rent any equipment you need if you're completing part of the project yourself. Buying equipment often costs more.

• Compare prices. Your contractor gets a discount on many products, but you might pay less if you shop around and buy your own materials.

• Keep the shape simple if you're building an addition. A square foundation costs less than one with lots of angles. To add interest inside, angle interior walls, leave ceilings open to the roofline, and pay attention to finish details such as molding.

• Plan around features that are costly to move, such as plumbing stacks, heat runs, and chimneys. You'll reduce costs if you leave exterior openings (doors, windows, chimneys, plumbing stacks, kitchen and bathroom vent fans, and the like) in their original locations and cut back on the number of bump-outs and bays.

Floor Plan Insight

Use these tips to visualize your new space and make it work better for you.

Not everyone can "see" what their remodeled room will look and feel like. If blueprints look like hieroglyphics to you, ask your architect or designer to give you a simpler drawing. Most people also appreciate a three-dimensional color drawing, complete with furniture, architectural features, light-

ing, and landscaping sketched in.

Your design pro also might offer to let you "tour" your project before it's constructed using a computer-aided design (CAD) program. This software lets you experiment with configurations and view the space in three dimensions from different vantage points.

Other people find it more helpful to outline the shape and size of a room or addition using stakes and

Plan enough storage in your remodeling project to ease your existing storage crunch. A closet organizing company reorganized and "stretched" the space in this 9×12-foot closet. New drawers organize socks and underwear; a new island makes for easy folding and packing and provides bins for dirty clothes.

string in the yard. If you're considering an addition, stake it out in the proposed final location of the project. If you're staking out a room that uses existing space within the house, you can stake it out anywhere in your yard (or garage or driveway) where you have sufficient room. Use objects such as lawn furniture and cardboard boxes to represent household furniture, cabinetry, and appliances within the staked out area. Walk around the "space" and see how it feels. Try to imagine using it on a daily basis. Note the locations of windows and doors as well as any views or obstacles. As you study the floor plan and any other visual aids that your design professional offers you, consider whether the new space works for your lifestyle or pattern of activity. For example, if your kids always drop their backpacks at the kitchen door and head for the refrigerator, is there a storage area by the door for their gear?

Note, too, whether there is ample room for the number of people who will be using the room at the same time. Traffic should be able to flow without crowding work areas or other people.

Make sure there is room for your furniture in an arrangement that you like. This is also a good time to consider the locations of light switches, electrical outlets, and fixtures.

After you study the floor plan or model in conjunction with how you live day-to-day, you'll be able to make adjustments as necessary to create a living space tailored to fit.

Make way for...
A Multipurpose Mudroom
Located near a back entrance or between the garage and kitchen, a mudroom handles muddy boots and grimy fingers with easy-care, wipe-

clean surfaces. But a mudroom can handle more than just mud.

The planning stage of a family room, kitchen, or garage—whether it's an addition or reworked space—is an ideal time to work in a service area that performs a number of valuable functions.

Store outdoor gear. From winter wraps to summer sports equipment, think of the things you could stash in a multipurpose mudroom and plan storage accordingly.

Serve as a laundry. A service area located beside the kitchen is often a good location for the washer and dryer. To save space while increasing function, include a fold-down ironing board in your plans. (Many newer homes are taking advantage of the latest generation of quieter appliances to locate a laundry just about anywhere for convenience.)

Handle hobbies. If you have a special pastime but lack an organized area for enjoying it, consider including a table and bench for sewing, working on crafts, or wrapping gifts. Many homeowners are relocating phone and bookkeeping desks from kitchens to mudrooms in order to keep clutter corralled and out of sight.

Pamper a pet. The "shower" located beside the laundry area in the 10×15-foot mudroom on page 127 is ideal for hang-drying freshly washed clothing (from a retractable rod) and serving as a shallow pet-washing basin for the family dog.

Make way for...
Spacious Closets
Allow enough space in your floor plan to create the perfect closet, whether that means making the storage you have work harder or finding enough square footage for a new closet.

If you're springing for a major remodeling venture, be sure to address storage needs. Enhance or increase your present storage to make your new space even more worthwhile. Here are some strategies:

Make do. Hardware and home improvement centers are full of ready-to-install racks, dividers, and storage drawers to help you get the most from the closet space you have. Most offer brochures that show standard closet sizes and arrangements and provide suggestions for improving them. If the storage solutions they offer don't solve your storage dilemma, consider hiring a professional closet designer to help you meet your specific needs. If you live in or near a metropolitan area, visit a local closet organizing store. Most employ a staff professional who can visit your house, make suggestions, and draw up a plan. The fee for the visit and the plan are sometimes waived if you purchase your organizing tools from the store and allow them to do the installation.

Make new. When planning a closet, consider annexing space from an adjacent room. If the room you're remodeling shares a wall with a guest bedroom closet, simply add another door so you can access the closet from both rooms. If you're planning an addition, consider adding a few extra feet to create all the storage space you need. If you have an underutilized guest room in your home, you may want to consider turning it into a combination dressing area and closet as shown *opposite*. Few people complain about having too much storage space, but many, many people complain about having too little.

Last Chance!

Is remodeling really the right solution for you? Answer this question with your head, your heart, and your wallet.

Times change and so do household needs. During one season in life, a two-bedroom ranch may be adequate. But when kids come or another adult moves in, a space crunch arises. The question then becomes, Should I improve what I have or move? While there is no wrong answer, your decision depends on your needs, your wants, your style, and your budget. Review your options by asking yourself these questions:

What kind of house do I need? Is yours a large family that needs a big kitchen and lots of bedrooms? Do you entertain a lot? With those questions in mind, consider your present home. Is the arrangement close enough to what you want that adding on a room or two will provide all the space you need? Can you remove a wall between the kitchen and family room to create the great-room you've always wanted? Or would the space require so many changes that adding on makes more sense?

Can my present house accept an addition? Not all homes are worth remodeling. The inadequacies of an older home can be magnified by the new materials used in an addition. Existing aspects that seemed passable, such as the roof, siding, and windows, may suddenly look worn and tired. Electrical, heating, and plumbing systems serving the house may not be adequate to support an addition and may require modification or replacement. If you're contemplating an addition, work with your architect or designer to get a clear picture of all it entails. Will you be satisfied with the balance between the old and new, or will you create future contracting projects and budget woes?

What makes the most sense in terms of investment? Is it wiser to invest $20,000 or $30,000 in your present home or sell the house and invest the equity in a new home? If you have a small house in a neighborhood of mansions, updating may substantially increase its worth. On the flip side, a $300,000 house sitting in a $200,000 neighborhood reduces the possibility of any return on your investment. If you plan to sell your house a few years down the road, consider saving your improvements for your next home. If you plan to live in a home for the rest of your life, let your heart—not your investment portfolio—decide which is the best solution.

Remodeling Survival Tips

When your home transforms into a construction zone, the mess makes you wonder if your life will ever return to normal. To ensure that the inconveniences of a remodeling project don't become major headaches, discuss your concerns with your contractor before work begins.

At your preconstruction meeting (where you, the contractor, and the construction manager are present), ask for an overview of the entire construction process. Together, develop a plan to minimize disruption to the household.

Discuss what the contractor will do to control dust. Most contractors

---

Hidden Costs
When comparing the expense of buying a new home to that of remodeling, review this list of commonly overlooked costs. Any of these items can reach into the thousands of dollars.

RELOCATING/BUYING NEW:
- Real estate agent commissions
- Closing costs
- Moving costs
- Draperies and other window coverings
- New and appropriate furnishings
- Landscaping
- Neighborhood association fees

REMODELING:
- Loan costs
- Correcting unexpected structural problems
- Updating existing utility systems
- Redecorating and furnishing
- Moving porches, patios, and decks to accommodate an addition

tape a plastic barrier at doorways to reduce the amount of dust that escapes from the construction zone. Some also may tape off heat registers and change the furnace filters daily, especially when sanding drywall.
Request floor protection. Request that walkways and carpeted areas that lead to the construction zone be covered with drop cloths or plastic runners.

Realize that noise is inevitable. Ask workers to arrive and leave at reasonable hours. Understand that if you set shorter work days, you may lengthen the duration of the project.
Coordinate schedules. Let the contractor know in advance if there are any times, such as holidays or special family events, when your house will be off-limits to project work.

Set up camp.
Make temporary changes to minimize disruption and inconvenience. If you're remodeling the kitchen, for example, move the refrigerator, the coffeepot, and the microwave to the dining room to reduce the problems that come with limited accessibility.

Index